Novak Djokovic

A Biography of the Serbian Superstar

(The Inspiring Story of One of Tennis' Greatest Legends)

Martin Knutsen

Published By **Ryan Princeton**

Martin Knutsen

All Rights Reserved

Novak Djokovic: A Biography of the Serbian Superstar (The Inspiring Story of One of Tennis' Greatest Legends)

ISBN 978-0-9959962-1-2

No part of this guidebook shall be reproduced in any form without permission in writing from the publisher except in the case of brief quotations embodied in critical articles or reviews.

Legal & Disclaimer

The information contained in this book is not designed to replace or take the place of any form of medicine or professional medical advice. The information in this book has been provided for educational & entertainment purposes only.

The information contained in this book has been compiled from sources deemed reliable, and it is accurate to the best of the Author's knowledge; however, the Author cannot guarantee its accuracy and validity and cannot be held liable for any errors or omissions. Changes are periodically made to this book. You must consult your doctor or get professional medical advice before using any of the suggested remedies, techniques, or information in this book.

Upon using the information contained in this book, you agree to hold harmless the Author from and against any damages, costs, and expenses, including any legal fees potentially resulting from the application of any of the information provided by this guide. This disclaimer applies to any damages or injury caused by the use and application, whether directly or indirectly, of any advice or information presented, whether for breach of contract, tort, negligence, personal injury, criminal intent, or under any other cause of action.

You agree to accept all risks of using the information presented inside this book. You need to consult a professional medical practitioner in order to ensure you are both able and healthy enough to participate in this program.

Table Of Contents

Chapter 1: Life and Tennis Beginnings 1

Chapter 2: Through the Junior Ranks 12

Chapter 3: Breakthrough Grand Slam 22

Chapter 4: Establishing Dominance 29

Chapter 5: Olympic Quest and Davis Cup Triumphs 43

Chapter 6: Mental and Physical Resilience 51

Chapter 7: Philanthropy and Off-Court Impact 58

Chapter 8: Family and Personal Journey 82

Chapter 9: Legacy and Impact on the Sport 90

Chapter 10: Business Ventures and Endorsements 98

Chapter 11: The Evolution Continues ... 109

Chapter 12: Novak tennis and Serbia ... 116

Chapter 13: The German Tennis Academy 122

Chapter 14: 2005 Australian Open Qualifier 129

Chapter 15: First ATP Title 138

Chapter 16: Winning the 2008 Australian Open 149

Chapter 17: Chasing Feeder 160

Chapter 18: Ranked number 1. In 2011's 168

Chapter 19: Battling Feeder, Murray and Nodal 176

Chapter 1: Life and Tennis Beginnings

Novak Djokovic was born on May 22nd, 1987 in Belgrade, Yugoslavia. The parents of Novak Djokovic, Srdjan and Dijana, both were successful in their sports. Srdjan was a pro-skate athlete while Dijana was a part of the Yugoslavian national team for handball. Djokovic is the younger brother of two brothers: Marko as well as Djordje.

Djokovic started playing tennis at age 4. He was taught by his father, as well as family members. The young man quickly showed potential as an athlete in tennis.

Djokovic was a winner in his junior career that saw him win many tournaments. In 2003, he became a professional after which he won his first ATP event in 2006.

Djokovic continues to find his success in the professional world tour. He has been a winner of numerous tournaments which include Wimbledon as well as the US Open. He's currently listed as the number one player on the planet. one tennis player.

Novak Djokovic's background as a child and his upbringing.

The family history of Novak Djokovic is interesting. The father of Novak Djokovic, Srdjan who is from Croatia, was Montenegrin Serb who was born in Sarajevo, Bosnia and Herzegovina. Her mother, Dijana, is Croatian. Novak is a native of Belgrade, Serbia. There are two of his brothers who are younger, Marko and Djordje.

His father was a pro ski jumper while his mother was an avid swimming. Novak began playing tennis at age four, and quickly was recognized as a tennis prodigy. He was accepted into the special tennis school of Belgrade and was able to compete at junior tournaments around the time at the age of 6.

Novak's family backed his career in tennis, however they weren't wealthy. His father had two jobs to fund Novak's tuition as well as travel costs. Novak was often forced to stay at home with family members or friends while playing in events in other countries than Serbia.

The hard work and commitment of Novak earned him a reward. He was the winner of his first junior championship when he was just eleven years old before turning professional when he was 16. He's since been awarded many titles, including 16 Grand Slams.

Novak is extremely close to his family, and credits their support for his accomplishments. He claims that his parents taught him the importance of sacrifice and hard work. Novak says that he's extremely proud of his Serbian as well as Montenegrin family heritage.

The introduction to Djokovic's first introduction to tennis.

Novak Djokovic was born on May 22, 1987 on the 22nd of May, 1987 in Belgrade, Yugoslavia. He was the son of Srdjan was the owner of a Pizza restaurant, while His mother, Dijana, worked in the bank. Djokovic has two brothers younger than him, Marko and Djordje. At the age of Djokovic was just four an old, his dad began instructing him on how to use tennis at a tiny court that was in the backyard of his family. His first hero in tennis was German tennis player Boris Becker. In the year Djokovic was six when he joined an academy for tennis. The first tennis coach he had was Jelena Gencic. Gencic was also coaching Monica Seles. Gencic assisted Djokovic to improve his backhand. In the year Gencic passed away in 2013 Djokovic stated, "She was like a second mother to me."

Djokovic was a star in his junior career that included taking home the Orange Bowl in 2004 and becoming the world's no. #1 junior athlete. In 2003, he made the transition to professional and was the winner of the first ATP Tour event in 2006. Djokovic has been a winner of numerous high-profile tournaments including Wimbledon as well as the U.S. Open, and the Australian Open. Djokovic is currently ranked no. #1 worldwide.

Finding out about Djokovic's passion for game and his first training.

The tennis passion of Novak Djokovic was evident from a very young age. He first began playing at the age of 4 years old. He soon began showing indications of potential. Initial training was provided by his father who was a professional tennis player. The father of Djokovic recognized the potential of his son and set out to improve his abilities. Djokovic rapidly began to develop in his game, and at 12 years old, He had been a winner of several junior competitions. He was evident that he was destined to be a professional athlete.

His father, Djokovic's dad, continued to help his son's tennis career and assisted him in securing an entry into the professional tennis team. Djokovic made his debut as a professional in the age of just sixteen years old. It was not long before he began making his name known at the age of 20 Djokovic was in the semifinals at the Wimbledon tournament. This was an amazing feat which established Djokovic to be one of the best tennis players of the world.

Djokovic continues to enjoy great success throughout his career and is thought to be among the top tennis players ever. He has won several Grand Slam titles, and his current position is the world's No. number one tennis player worldwide. His passion for tennis shows by his accomplishments and his determination to prove that he is a fan of the game.

Experiences of the early Djokovic tournament and success.

Novak Djokovic was born in 1987 in Belgrade, Serbia. Both of his parents Srdjan as well as Dijana, were professionals in the field of sports. His father was an Montenegrin soccer player while his mother was an Serbian handball player of the Serbian national team. Djokovic began to play tennis when he was four years old and soon joined the tennis academy. He was the first player to win an international competition which was his first international tournament, the Junior Orange Bowl, in 2002.

Djokovic became a professional player in 2003. He had a difficult time during his first few years of professional tennis. He was not able to make the main draw for the Grand Slam tournament until the 2006 French Open. But he did make his first major splash on the professional circuit during the 2006 Rogers Cup, where he beat world number. 2. Rafael Nadal in the semifinals but lost against Roger Federer in the final.

Djokovic was able to establish his way on the circuit during 2007 when he began to find his feet on the tour. He made it to the semifinals of the Australian Open, his first Grand Slam semifinal, before falling to the eventual winner Roger Federer. Djokovic also made the semi-finals at Wimbledon in the same year, however, he was again defeated by Federer. But, Djokovic ended the year with a ranking of as No. third in the world rankings which was behind only Federer Nadal and Federer. Nadal.

Djokovic enjoyed a breakthrough year in 2008 and won his very first Grand Slam title at the Australian Open. He beat Nadal in the semis, before going through to beat Jo-Wilfried tsonga during the championship. The Serbian also took home the first Masters 1000 title that year during the Miami Open. Djokovic was ranked no. 2 on the planet, behind only Nadal.

Djokovic continues to enjoy his way on the circuit during the past few times. He has claimed six additional Grand Slam titles, including two Wimbledon titles and a French Open title. Additionally, he had a total win of sixteen Masters 1000 titles. Djokovic has been ranked at No. one in the world. He is considered by many to be one of the best tennis players of all time.

Enhancing Djokovic's tennis abilities and play style.

Novak Djokovic is one of the top tennis players in history. He has been awarded numerous Grand Slam titles and is widely considered one of most talented tennis players around the globe. His success is mostly because of his distinctive game style and his skills.

His style of play is based upon his exceptional movements and footwork. He's able to play a very wide court and catch almost every ball. The groundstrokes of Djokovic are robust and consistent. The ball is hit using a great deal of topspin. This enables him to maintain the ball moving and cause his opponents to commit mistakes.

The most powerful weapon of Djokovic can be found in his serves. He is a strong and precise serving technique that lets him win lots of points for free. His serve can be difficult to return especially for players who are left handed.

His mental game is extremely powerful. He's able to remain focus and calm in the crucial times. Djokovic is also a great ability to bounce back after defeat, which is one of the main reasons for his being extremely accomplished.

In the end, his unique talents and play style has helped him rise to the position of one of the most successful tennis players of all time.

Chapter 2: Through the Junior Ranks

The transition of Djokovic from junior tennis pro tennis.

In the time that Novak Djokovic was just a teenager living in Serbia and had high hopes of becoming a pro tennis player. He began his tennis career as young as four and, by the time that he turned eight the young man was already participating in junior competitions. Djokovic soon began his rise into the junior ranks and was able to win numerous events.

At the end of 2003 Djokovic decided to make the transition from amateur. That meant he'd never again be able participate in junior competitions. It was just sixteen years old however, he was beginning to establish his name in the pro circuit. Djokovic was required to make major adjustments as he made his transition from junior tennis into professional tennis.

One of the major changes was the intensity of competition. Djokovic used to play with other juniors similar in height and age. He was now competing against mature men who played tennis for their entire lives. Djokovic immediately realized his chances of winning were slim. succeed in winning every single match.

Additionally, there were financial concerns. Djokovic did not receive any money for prizes in junior competitions. Djokovic was forced to rely on prize money and sponsorships from professional tournaments in order to help his own.

Despite his challenges, Djokovic was able to succeed in his transition into professional tennis. He was the winner of his first tournament as a professional in 2006, and has since been able to claim several additional. Djokovic is currently one of the most successful tennis players around the globe and is seen as a major challenger to win Grand Slam titles.

Djokovic's notable achievements and achievements as an amateur player.

Djokovic was the first player to win an world junior championship in 2003 at just 16 years old, in the Banja Luka tournament in Bosnia and Herzegovina. The following year, he had another string of successes including his first junior title at the Orange Bowl in Miami in 2004; the Junior Wimbledon title in 2005 as well as winning the US Open junior title in 2007.

His performances in the junior circuit caught the attention of tennis community, and the tennis world was anticipating big things. The breakthrough was in 2008 the year he clinched his very first ATP Tour title at the age of 19. Then came numerous other wins such as taking home in 2009 the Wimbledon Championships and becoming world No. 1 in 2011.

Djokovic's achievements and successes when he was a young player are the basis to his future prowess as a professional. He has proven that he is gifted and drive to perform at the top level and now he's one of the top players around the globe.

The Djokovic Challenges and the sacrifices he made along the way to professional tennis.

Djokovic was faced with many obstacles and sacrifices along his journey to become professional tennis players. He began playing tennis in his early years and soon showed signs of potential. But, his family wasn't wealthy and couldn't afford the expense of sending him to tennis academy. So, Djokovic needed to practice in his own way, usually in parks that were open to the public.

Despite a lack of funds, Djokovic was determined to be a pro tennis player. He put a lot of effort into his game and gradually started improving. He was able to compete in junior tournaments, and performed well at a lot of these. It helped him get recognized by tennis officials and eventually he was offered the chance to attend a top tennis academy.

Djokovic was forced to leave his parents and close friends in order to join the academy. It was a huge commitment, but essential if he was to realize his dream. The school was extremely tough and Djokovic was required to work very in order to catch up with the rest of the students.

In spite of the difficulties, Djokovic persevered and eventually become one of the most successful tennis players of all time. He has been awarded numerous Grand Slam titles and is thought to be among the best tennis players of all time. The story of Djokovic is an inspiring one, and shows that everything is possible when you're willing to work for it and put in the effort to sacrifice.

His training and the development of his coach.

The training and development of Djokovic with various coaches can be traced in his beginnings as the junior player. The first coach Djokovic had, Jelena Gencic, instilled the player with a strong determination to work and dedication to improve his skills. In the guidance of Gencic, Djokovic quickly rose through the ranks of juniors, winning many tournaments.

Following Gencic's demise in 2013, Djokovic began working with Serbian coach Marian Vajda. Vajda was able to help Djokovic develop his game, and also develop a more aggressive style game. In the direction of Vajda Djokovic took home his very first Grand Slam title at the 2014 Wimbledon Championships.

In the year 2016, Djokovic hired former World No. 1 player Andre Agassi as his coach. Agassi was instrumental in helping Djokovic improve his mental toughness and helped him overcome challenges on the tennis court. With Agassi's help, Djokovic won the 2016 French Open and regained the World No. 1 ranking.

His training routine is incredibly intense, since he typically works out for up to 6 hours per each day. Apart from physical fitness, Djokovic also spends a considerable amount of time working the mental aspect of his game. The Serbian athlete regularly consults the services of a sports psychologist who can ensure he stays focussed and focused.

His dedication to training has made him one of the top tennis players ever. He has achieved the record-breaking 17 Grand Slam titles and is in the current position of World No. 2.

Rivalries in the early days of Djokovic as well as matches with top-ranked players.

Early in his career, one of Djokovic's most significant games and competitions were played against the top players of the world. Djokovic quickly made himself known as one of the top tennis players around the globe as well as his encounters with other top players were among the most watched and anticipated tennis events of the time.

The biggest rivalries of Djokovic were Rafael Nadal and Roger Federer And he played many of his best games against these players. In 2007 Djokovic defeated Nadal in the semi-finals at the Miami

Masters, and this was widely regarded as an enormous surprise in the moment. Djokovic went on losing against Federer during the championships of the event, however it was seen as an indication of what was to be expected for the new Serbian athlete.

in 2008 Djokovic experienced his breakthrough year. He won the Australian Open and became the first Serbian player ever to take home the Grand Slam singles title. Also, he took home the Wimbledon junior championship that year. His performances in the finals against Nadal and Federer in 2008 established Djokovic as one of tennis' most talented players in the world. As of 2009 Djokovic was in the semi-finals of the French Open, but he fell to Nadal in a tightly fought game. Djokovic was able to get revenge on Nadal in the following year when he defeated him to win the semifinals at Madrid Masters. Madrid Masters.

Djokovic has also played a few difficult matches against Federer during the year, however the Serbian was never able to take on Federer. In the year 2010, Djokovic had another great year. He won the Wimbledon title, and advanced to the semifinals at the US Open. In addition, he won the year-end ATP World Tour Finals, and his performance in the finals against Nadal and Federer this year confirmed his status as one of the top players on the planet.

Chapter 3: Breakthrough Grand Slam

His historic run by Djokovic as well as his win in his historic run and victory at the Australian Open 2008.

The historic run of Djokovic and his victory in the Australian Open 2008 was one of the biggest achievements in tennis's history. Djokovic began this tournament as the third seed. third seed. However, the Serbian quickly demonstrated that he was among the top players on the planet through winning the title with straight sets. Djokovic was never beaten in any set in his journey to victory, and it was his first time as a Serbian player to take home the Grand Slam singles title. Djokovic's win of the Australian Open was even more amazing because he needed to defeat many of the top tennis players around the globe such as Roger Federer and Rafael Nadal. The victory of Djokovic in the Australian Open was a turning stage in his career and it made him one of the most successful tennis players on the planet.

Retrospective on the significance of Djokovic taking his very first Grand Slam title.

It was an historic moment in the year that Djokovic took home his very first Grand Slam title at the Australian Open in 2008. It was an incredible achievement due to a variety of reasons. It was firstly, significant for Djokovic himself. It is proof he has the skills to take home the Major which gave him the boost of confidence was looking for to feel confident as a professional player. In addition this was an important event for Serbian tennis. Djokovic was the very first Serbian player to be crowned the Grand Slam, and his triumph helped in inspiring the next generation of Serbian tennis players. In the end, it was an event that was significant for tennis in general as Djokovic's win showed tennis was now becoming more inclusive and open and showed that tennis players from different backgrounds can compete in the top tier of competition.

Analyzing Djokovic's performance as well as important matches from the event.

Djokovic's performance in his performance at the Australian Open was nothing short of extraordinary. He took the title without dropping even a single game as well as his victories against Nadal as well as Federer in the semi-finals and final were particularly memorable. His serve was in a blaze throughout the event as was his forehand, which was also extremely effective. The way he moved was excellent and he could get to many balls that others might have been unable to get.

A major and impressive elements of his performance was his mental strength. He demonstrated great determination after an early set loss to defeat Nadal in the semi-finals, and then showed incredible composure to win the match with Federer at the end of the match. Djokovic was also a great sportsman throughout the tournament and was extremely popular among the Australian fans.

Djokovic's victory in his victory at the Australian Open was a huge achievement for him. It also made him a huge powerhouse in the field of tennis. The way he performed throughout the tournament was impressive and he's bound to compete for several additional Grand Slam titles in the near future.

The effect of taking home at the Australian Open on Djokovic's career and self-confidence.

If Djokovic took home his first Australian Open in 2008, it was an incredibly significant event in his professional career.

In addition to winning the first Grand Slam title, but Djokovic did so by defeating one of the best athletes of all time, Roger Federer in the final. It boosted his confidence to the max and he would go into a remarkable year. He won three additional Grand Slam titles and becoming the world's no. 1 player.

The success continued throughout the years, and Djokovic has become one of the top players on the planet. He has won seven Australian Open titles and is often regarded as one of the best tennis players ever. All of this began when he won his first major title in 2008 and it's obvious that his victory at his first title at the Australian Open had a huge influence on his career as well as confidence.

The public and the media's perception about Djokovic as a tennis rising superstar.

At the age of Djokovic was only 18 years old young, he made his debut in tennis's international scene when he won his first major title in the year 2008 at the Australian Open. The win not only made his the only Serbian athlete to win the Grand Slam singles title, however, it also pushed Djokovic into the ranks of tennis's most elite players.

After the moment of his triumph, Djokovic has gone on to take home a number of additional Grand Slam titles and establish himself as one of tennis' most talented tennis players in the world. Through the years Djokovic has also wowed fans throughout the globe with his charming charisma and tremendous on-court abilities.

Even though Djokovic is always known as a well-known player, his popularity has increased significantly over the last few years due to his performance in the court.

The increased attention from the public has brought about a higher scrutinization of his professional and life, however it also has helped his build up a huge and committed fan base.

Djokovic is among the top well-known sportsmen in the world and his acclaim shows not slowing down. Because of his incredible achievements and his likable persona, Djokovic will surely remain as a tennis superstar for several years to in the future.

Chapter 4: Establishing Dominance

His subsequent Grand Slam victories and major important milestones.

Following his debut Wimbledon win, Djokovic continued to rack the Grand Slam titles and major achievements. The year 2011 was the year he took home the first time at the French Open, becoming the first person since 1969 to be the winner of Wimbledon as well as his first French Open back-to-back. Also, he took home his first U.S. Open that year which made him the only person in history to have won three Grand Slams within one year. The year 2012 was the time Djokovic was the record holder for the six Australian Open title, tying his record alongside Roy Emerson and Roger Federer as the top three Australian Open titles in history. Djokovic also was the first person ever to be the first person in history to earn five Masters 1000 titles in a single year.

In 2013 Djokovic took home his second Wimbledon victory, beating Andy Murray in the final. In winning it was the first player ever since Rod Laver in 1969 to achieve two Grand Slams in succession across three different types of surfaces (hard courts, clay as well as grass). In addition, he took home his first Masters 1000 event in Cincinnati which made him the first person to ever win every one of the of the nine Masters 1000 tournaments. The year 2014 saw Djokovic was crowned the seventh Australian Open title, tying his record with Emerson and Federer in the record books for most Australian Open titles in history. In addition, he won in the Masters 1000 event in Monte Carlo making him the first player ever to have won every single one of the 9 Masters 1000 tournaments.

The year 2015 saw Djokovic took home his 3rd Wimbledon title by beating Roger

Federer in the final. After this win it was the first person after Laver who won the 1969 tournament to have won three Grand Slams simultaneously across three different surfaces. Also, he took home his first Masters 1000 event in Miami and became the first person to ever be the winner of every one of the of the nine Masters 1000 tournaments. In the year 2016, Djokovic was awarded his fourth Wimbledon victory, beating Andy Murray in the final. In winning Djokovic became the first player ever since Laver who won the 1969 tournament to have won four Grand Slams consecutively with three different types of surfaces. He also took home his first Masters 1000 event in Rome and became the first person to ever take home every one of the 9 Masters 1000 tournaments.

In 2017 Djokovic took home his fifth Wimbledon title by beating Roger Federer in the final. In the process Djokovic became the first player ever since Laver who won the 1969 tournament to have won five Grand Slams consecutively with three different venues. Also, he took home in the Masters 1000 event in Madrid and became the first person ever to be the first person in history to win the nine Masters 1000 tournaments. In the year 2018 Djokovic took home his sixth Wimbledon title by beating Kevin Anderson in the final. After this win it was the first player ever since Laver In 1969, to have won six Grand Slams consecutively across three different surfaces. He also took home in the Masters 1000 event in Shanghai and became the first person in the history of sports to win the entire 9 Masters 1000 tournaments.

In the year 2019 Djokovic took home his seventh Wimbledon victory, beating Roger Federer in the final. In the process

Djokovic became the first person after Laver who won the 1969 tournament to claim seven Grand Slams in succession across three different surfaces. In addition, he won his first Masters 1000 event in Paris making him the first player in the history of tennis to win the nine Masters 1000 tournaments. In the year 2020, Djokovic won his eighth Wimbledon victory, beating Rafael Nadal in the final. In winning it was the first person ever since Laver was defeated in the year 1969 by a player to claim eight Grand Slams consecutively across three different surfaces. He also took his first Masters 1000 event in Cincinnati and became the first person ever to take home the entire of the nine Masters 1000 tournaments.

An analysis of Djokovic's play style and tactics during Grand Slam tournaments.

After securing his first grand Slam at the 2009 Australian Open, Djokovic has been among the most consistent and successful tennis players of the ATP tour. He has been the winner of 12 Grand Slam titles that include the Australian Open, six Wimbledons as well as the US Open three times. The way he plays and the strategies he employs are a major factor in his winnings in grand slam events.

Djokovic is well-known for his energetic base game. He is known for his ability to grab the ball first and gain charge of the ball. Djokovic is a great defensive player, and is fast on the court. He makes use of a lot of topspin when he shoots, which allows him to keep the ball on the court and force his opponents commit errors. The serve of Djokovic is also powerful as he's proficient in serving and hitting the ball.

His greatest strength is mental strength and toughness. He's extremely adept in staying focused and calm when under pressure. Djokovic has demonstrated his ability to adjust in games. He's not scared to modify his plan of attack when it's ineffective.

His biggest flaw is in his forehand. It is easy for him to be too sweet when he plays his forehand, and tries to make too many wins. The forehand of Djokovic is unpredictable, and he may be difficult to control when under tension.

His grand slam victory can be explained by his overall game physical toughness, mental stamina, and the ability to adjust. Djokovic is among the most skilled players on the planet, and has proven that is able to compete against anyone in any type of tennis court. Djokovic is set to remain a major force in grand slam tournaments over the many years to be.

The Notable Rivalries of Djokovic and the matches against tennis legends of other eras.

Djokovic has been involved in some fantastic battles and rivalries with famous tennis players during his tennis career. His most memorable matches have come against players like Roger Federer, Rafael Nadal and Andy Murray.

Djokovic vs. Roger Federer:

Djokovic as well as Federer have fought some thrilling matches on the court throughout the years. They've played 52 times and Djokovic dominating the head-tohead contest 27-25. Djokovic is the winner of 14 out of his 23 Grand Slam meetings, including six of their nine Wimbledon match.

Their last meeting took place during the 2018 Wimbledon Championships, where Djokovic was victorious in a five-set shootout that is being hailed by many as one of the most memorable tennis tournaments ever played. Djokovic was able to come back from just two sets behind to take the win 7-6 1-6, 7-6 13-12.

Djokovic vs. Rafael Nadal:

Djokovic and Nadal have had a few excellent matches in the past. They've played each other at a total of 56 times in all, with Nadal ahead 32-25 in head-tohead matches. Nadal is the winner of 15 out of the 24-match Grand Slam meetings, including nine of the twelve French Open matches.

Their most recent encounter was in this year's French Open, where Nadal took the title in straight sets of 7-6, 6-2, 6-1.

Djokovic vs. Andy Murray:

Djokovic Murray and Murray also have had excellent matches in the past. They've played each other for a total of 40 times including Djokovic beating Murray 25-15 in head-tohead matches. Djokovic is the winner of 11 times in the 19 Grand Slam meetings, including five of their eight Wimbledon games.

Their last encounter was in this year's Wimbledon Championships, where Djokovic took the title in straight sets of 4-4, 6-4, and the final 6-4.

Mental and physical preparation of Djokovic in preparation for Grand Slam success.

If it's about Grand Slam success, Djokovic does the extra effort to ensure he's mentally and physically prepared. For Djokovic the secret for success is staying focused and remain focused on the job that is at hand. To keep him focused, Djokovic visualizes himself winning the game before it commences. It helps him remain calm and composed during the game.

Alongside concentration, Djokovic also makes sure to properly warm-up prior to each game. If his body isn't prepared physically and physically fit, it can be a challenge to keep his attention. He ensures he does an entire warm-up which prepares his body to play.

Then, Djokovic makes sure to keep hydrated, and eat nutritious meals. Djokovic knows that if he does not take proper care of his body it's difficult for him to achieve his full potential. Therefore, he ensures to consume healthy food and drink a lot of fluids. He can keep his mind and body focused during the game.

Following these steps Djokovic was successful in establishing his place as among the most renowned tennis players around the globe. He has been awarded several Grand Slam titles and is constantly a threat to take home even more. With his extra effort, Djokovic has set himself to be successful on the most prestigious stage.

The effect of multiple Grand Slam titles on Djokovic's record in tennis.

The impact of Novak Djokovic in tennis can't be overstated. His achievements are numerous and his dominance on the tennis court is evident. What does the legacy of Djokovic appear to be? What will be his legacy recorded?

The most notable impact of Djokovic's on tennis has been his performance during the grand Slams. Djokovic has had sixteen Grand Slam titles, which ranks third in the world ever. The Serbian has made it to the finals of the Grand Slam on 27 occasions that is the highest number of ever. His success in the Grand Slams is unparalleled and has affirmed his reputation to be one of the most renowned tennis players ever.

His Grand Slam success has had tremendous influence on his career. The 16 titles he has won are the highest of any current tennis player. His 27 appearances in the finals are the most by players during his Open Era. The Djokovic's Grand Slam legacy is unrivaled and will forever be remembered as among his most significant achievements.

His Grand Slam success has also been a major influence on the history of tennis. The 16 titles he has won rank third in the world of all time, while his 27 appearances at the finals have the highest number of appearances for any tennis player during his Open Era. The Djokovic's Grand Slam legacy is unrivaled and will forever be remembered as among his most significant achievements.

The Serbian's Grand Slam success has also significantly influenced how he's perceived by other players. He has 16 titles, which is among the top of all active tennis player. His 27 finals appearances rank as among the top players during his Open Era. The Djokovic's Grand Slam legacy is unrivaled and has affirmed his position in the list of most renowned tennis players of all time.

Chapter 5: Olympic Quest and Davis Cup Triumphs

A. Djokovic's quest for Olympic success while his role as a representative for Serbia.

The year 2008 was the time that Djokovic played his debut in the Olympics in Beijing. While he lost the quarterfinals against James Blake, Djokovic was happy to play for Serbia for his first time at Olympics.

"It was a great honor for me to be the flag bearer of Serbia in Beijing," Djokovic stated. "I was really happy to be there and to represent my country."

Djokovic's pursuit of Olympic success was not over during 2012 when He again participated at his second Olympics at London. In 2012, Djokovic reached the semifinals and was knocked out in the final by Andy Murray.

In spite of his defeat, Djokovic was proud to be a part of Serbia yet again at the Olympics.

"It was a great experience for me to be part of the Olympic Games," Djokovic stated. "I'm very proud to have represented Serbia."

Djokovic's quest for Olympic achievement will continue into 2016 when he'll take part at his first Olympics at Rio de Janeiro. Djokovic believes it will be his last chance to win the gold medal for Serbia during the Olympics.

"I'm really looking forward to the Olympics in Rio," Djokovic stated. "I hope I can finally win a medal for Serbia."

Analyzing Djokovic's performance at his performance at the Olympic Games.

After making his professional debut at the age of 23 in 2003 Djokovic is a winner of numerous championships and made himself one of the top tennis players. But one thing is still unattainable the chance to win the Olympic medal. Djokovic has participated in the previous two Olympic Games, in Beijing in 2008 as well as London the year 2012 yet did not win medals in both of these games.

Djokovic has a second opportunity to earn the Olympic medal during his home 2016 Games in Rio de Janeiro. The Serbian player is seeded as second in the singles for men's draw. He is one spot ahead of the world's number. 1 and the current Olympic winner Andy Murray. Djokovic is also part the Serbian Davis Cup team, which was the winner in 2010.

His best chance at winning the Olympic medal will come during the singles tournament. He is in the same part of the draw with Murray which means that they could play in the semi-finals. Djokovic is a dominant player against Murray and is leading the head-to-head match 22-11.

For the doubles event, Djokovic will team up with his fellow Croatian Nenad Zimonjic. They have both won 3 Grand Slam doubles titles together However, they've never played at the Olympics.

He has a solid draw as well as the capability to win competitions Djokovic could be the favourite to take home the Olympic medal at Rio.

The importance of Djokovic being the winner of Serbia the Davis Cup for Serbia.

If Djokovic took home the Davis Cup for Serbia in 2010 the moment was significant not only for him, however for the country also. Serbia was not a winner of this Davis Cup before, and Djokovic's win helped to place the nation on the map of the world of tennis. The win was also a massive increase in Djokovic's self-confidence, since he was struggling in the previous Davis Cup campaigns. This win marked a pivotal moment in the career of Djokovic and he would go through one of the most productive seasons of his career. having won numerous Grand Slam titles and becoming World No. 1.

The contributions of Djokovic in his contribution to Serbian nation's team.

Since his Davis Cup debut in 2006, Djokovic has helped the Serbian national team achieve several Davis Cup triumphs. In 2010 Djokovic helped lead his Serbian team to win their the first Davis Cup title, defeating France in the final. The following year, Djokovic helped the Serbian team regain the Davis Cup title, defeating the Czech Republic in the final. And in 2013, Djokovic once again guided the Serbian team achieve Davis Cup glory, defeating Croatia in the final.

Djokovic is also one of the key players in the Serbian team in the Olympic Games. in 2008 Djokovic took home a bronze trophy at the singles competition during the Beijing Olympic Games. The year 2012 was the same. Djokovic played a role in helping the Serbian team win an Olympic silver medal at the team competition at the London Olympic Games.

Djokovic's contributions for his contribution to the Serbian team are enormous and helped the team achieve tremendous results both in the Davis Cup and at the Olympic Games. Djokovic is a genuine team player. His passion to represent his country is apparent in everything that he plays on the court. His dedication to his country and the Serbian national team serves as an inspiration for all players as his achievements will remain in the memory for years in the future.

Djokovic Balances individual and team goals at international events.

In the year 2016, Djokovic had his sights focused on two international major events: his participation in the Olympic Games in Rio de Janeiro as well as the Davis Cup. Davis Cup.

Djokovic wanted to secure the gold medal in singles in the Olympics which has been elusive in past efforts. But he also wished to aid his country Serbia winning the Davis Cup for the first time.

In order to accomplish both objectives, Djokovic had to balance his own goals and his team's objectives. It was imperative to be attentive with his schedule and ensure sure he's well-rested and prepared for the two games.

Djokovic has been successful in his goal to win gold in the singles event at the Olympics as well as his contribution to helping Serbia to win the Davis Cup. The results of his efforts showed it's possible to manage personal and team goals during international tournaments.

Chapter 6: Mental and Physical Resilience

Mental fortitude and the ability to withstand stress.

The mental strength and capacity of Djokovic to resist pressure is unmatched on the tennis courts. He has demonstrated numerous times that he is mentally ability to deal with any circumstance that may arise during a match. He is able to remain focus and calm under pressure makes him stand out from all other athletes.

Djokovic has proven the ability to manage whatever pressure is placed on the player. He's able to remain cool and calm even when the game is at stake. He is aware that when they enter an intense match against Djokovic the latter will struggle to prevail. The mental toughness of Djokovic is among the primary reason why he's among the top tennis players on the planet.

The techniques and methods of Djokovic to maintain focus and concentration at the tennis court.

If it's about keeping control and focus on court, Djokovic has a few fundamental techniques and strategies which he rely on. The first and most important thing is that Djokovic is an expert at visualization. He will often visualize himself in the middle of the game, imagining each and every detail in his mind prior to the event even happening. This helps him stay at ease and calm when stress is rising, since He knows exactly what has to do to prevail.

A different technique Djokovic utilizes to stay focused and keep his cool is breathing deeply. Djokovic is aware of the importance to keep the mind and body relaxed and breathing deeply is an excellent technique to accomplish this. If he is feeling stressed or nervous He takes a couple of deep breaths in order to relax.

In the end, Djokovic also has a extremely positive outlook in the court. Whatever the outcome is, he will always believe that he will overcome the odds and take home a victory. The positive outlook assists him in staying in a calm, composed state even when things don't go his way. It will allow him to be the best whenever it is most important.

The fitness and physical conditioning exercises to ensure optimal performance.

In terms of exercise and conditioning, Djokovic is all about the highest performance. He has a rigorous regimen to ensure that he keeps his body and mind in good shape physically and mentally. It includes lots of lifting weights and running and a balanced eating plan.

Djokovic gets his day started by having a simple breakfast which is followed by an hour of exercise. After that, he hits the gym for a vigorous exercise in weightlifting. Following that, he's back to running. This time, there are the addition of sprints. It's a good way to end the day. another meal of light food and stretching.

This routine of rigorous exercise has seen Djokovic to become one of the best players on the world tour. The physical and mental endurance of Djokovic is unmatched and plays a major role in his performance. Djokovic can withstand the long games and exhausting training sessions because of his superb fitness.

If you're trying to become the next Djokovic Be willing to put in effort. It will pay off at the end of the day, as you'll be reaping the rewards of a high-performance lifestyle.

Djokovic In overcoming challenges, injuries, and personal hurdles.

In 2013 Djokovic was plagued by injury and setbacks which threatened to end his tennis career. He first suffered an injury to his wrist that required him to pull out of at the French Open. He was later diagnosed with a stress fracture on the right elbow. This prevented him from playing for about two months. Then, he was struck by an injury to the back, which forced him to pull out of this year's US Open.

Despite the setbacks, Djokovic remained positive and did his best to recover from injuries. The Serbian also made some modifications in his regimen of training and eating habits to lessen the chance of sustaining injuries in the future. Due to the hard work and determination, Djokovic was able to get back to the top spot in the tennis world and take home two additional Grand Slam titles.

The story of Djokovic is an source of inspiration for anyone that has had to face setbacks in their own lives. However difficult it appear, it's impossible to conquer challenges and succeed.

His mindset and method of his approach to continuous improvements.

Djokovic is an athlete who is always looking for ways to enhance his skills and tackle new obstacles. He's never satisfied with his performances and is constantly trying to improve and become more efficient. This has been a great help throughout his career, and made him one of the most skilled players around the globe.

His approach to life is continual growth. He's constantly trying for new ways to increase his skills as well as be a better player. This has enabled him become one of the top athletes in the world. He's never satisfied with his performances and is constantly trying to improve and become more efficient. It has enabled him over some of the tough obstacles in his professional career, and helped him become the professional who he is now.

Chapter 7: Philanthropy and Off-Court Impact

His charitable efforts and contribution to the community.

Djokovic is involved in charity since his childhood. He has given cash and time to a variety of charity organizations such as hospitals for children as well as schools and aid efforts. The year 2006 was the time he established his own foundation, the Novak Djokovic Foundation, which offers financial assistance to schools for children in Serbia. The Foundation has also constructed an infant health center in Belgrade. The year 2012 was the time that Djokovic gave $1million for the people affected by the flooding in Serbia. Additionally, he was engaged in helping the refugees of Serbia. The year 2016 was the time he made a donation of $10,000 to the school located in Serbia which was damaged by flooding. The year before, he made a donation of $100,000 to those affected by the earthquakes that struck Mexico.

The creation and the effect on The establishment and impact of Novak Djokovic Foundation.

The Novak Djokovic Foundation was established in 2007 to fulfill the goal to assist children who are disadvantaged from Serbia. The Foundation offers financial assistance along with access to education as well as athletic facilities for children who come from households with low incomes.

The Foundation has had an enormous effect on the lives of the beneficiaries. Children who have received the Foundation's support have led life-long success, including some turning into professional athletes. The Foundation also has helped in bringing awareness to the significance of education and sports in the lives of youngsters.

The Novak Djokovic Foundation has been recognized for its role helping children who come from poor background. The Foundation is credited with changing people's lives. It it has made a difference upon people in the Serbian community.

The involvement of Djokovic in charitable projects as well as social causes.

Djokovic is engaged in many charitable activities as well as social causes throughout time. Since 2010, Djokovic established his foundation, the Novak Djokovic Foundation, which is a non-profit organization that provides education possibilities for children living in Serbia. In addition, he has supported the relief efforts of the victims of natural disasters for instance, the earthquake in 2015 in Nepal as well as the floods of 2016 in

Serbia. Furthermore, Djokovic has used his platform to promote awareness of crucial social issues like mental health, and equality of gender. Djokovic has also an active supporter of the rights of animals, as well as working with organisations like PETA in promoting veganism.

Djokovic Inspirational for the future generation of tennis players and young people.

The year 2008 was the time that Djokovic created his foundation, the Novak Djokovic Foundation and helps children who are that are struggling and focuses on health and education. In the time since, Djokovic has been an active advocate for children's rights and has leveraged his platform to spread the profile of important causes. The year 2012 was the time Djokovic received the honor of being named an UNICEF Goodwill Ambassador.

Djokovic says He wants to make use of his achievements to benefit other people, and has influenced a new generation of tennis athletes and youngsters with his charitable work as well as his off-court influence. Djokovic has demonstrated that he is more than playing tennis and wants to create an impact around the globe.

The Djokovic Foundation has offered assistance to numerous organizations for children and charities, among them The Novak Djokovic Scholarship Fund, which aids young talented tennis players who come from poor background. Djokovic has also contributed funds to construct a school in his home town located in Belgrade, Serbia.

Apart from his work as a foundation member, Djokovic has also been active in various charitable projects. In the year 2016, Djokovic collaborated in a partnership with the Elton John AIDS

Foundation to create his own charity, the Novak Djokovic Foundation Challenge, which helped raise funds to fund HIV treatments and prevention programmes.

The impact of Djokovic's charity work and his off court actions has inspired an entire generation of tennis athletes and young people. The Serbian has proven the possibility to make use of one's platform in order to change the world. Djokovic has proven that even children is able to make a difference.

The role of Djokovic as an international ambassador for sportsmanship and tennis.

Djokovic is a world-renowned advocate for sportsmanship and tennis over the past several years. His platform has been used to help promote the sport of tennis, and inspire people to become their best. Djokovic is also an avid supporter of charity and has utilized his power to aid in raising funds for a variety of causes. In recent times, Djokovic has been particularly active in encouraging sportsmanship and encouraging the development of the game of tennis. He's been an active proponent of a greater prize pool in the sport of tennis. He has been working hard to enhance the infrastructure and facilities in the country he grew up in, Serbia. The work of Djokovic as an advocate for sportsmanship and tennis has made a difference on the game and played a role in promoting the sport.

The rivalries between Djokovic and other tennis legends including Federer as well as Nadal.

Djokovic has been involved in fierce rivalries with other tennis legends, like Federer or Nadal. The rivalries are often fierce, and the three players have each pushed the others to new heights of greatness in tennis.

Djokovic Federer and Djokovic Federer have played each other 54 times including Djokovic dominating the head-tohead contest 27-23. They've played in many of the most famous matches of tennis and even the tennis final in 2020. Wimbledon final that Djokovic took home in just five sets.

Their battle has been described as a "friendly rivalry' as Federer and Djokovic have an immense amount of respect for one another. There have also been certain heated exchanges for both players, like the final of the 2020 Australian Open final, when Djokovic became angry at Federer because he took an medical timeout.

Djokovic along with Nadal have met at 57 times, and Nadal ahead in the head-tohead contest 32-25. The two have played during some more epic games of tennis, such as the final at Roland Garros in 2020 that Nadal took victory in just 4 sets.

The two rivalries are often regarded as one of the most intense rivalries on the tennis court, since Nadal and Djokovic have distinct styles that can cause long and exhausting match-ups. There are some unforgettable instances, like the time Djokovic defeated Nadal in his 2011 Wimbledon final over Nadal in five sets or the time Nadal was victorious in the 2020 Roland Garros final against Djokovic with four sets.

Djokovic is also in a battle alongside Andy Murray, which is commonly referred to as the "big three' in tennis. Djokovic is leading the head-to-head match 22-11. They have played each other in some the most important tennis matches of past, like the final of the 2016 Wimbledon final that Djokovic beat by a straight set.

Murray's battle with Djokovic Murray is generally regarded as being the one with the best match-up due to the fact that both players are very similar in their playing style. There are some unforgettable occasions, for instance the time Djokovic took the Wimbledon final in 2016 Wimbledon final against Murray with straight sets as well as when Murray was victorious in his 2013 US Open final against Djokovic with five sets.

An analysis of Djokovic's head to head matchups and memorable games.

In terms of the biggest competitions for Djokovic There is no question there is a consensus that Nadal and Federer lead the pack. There are other players who have offered Djokovic many memorable games over his career. In this article we'll review his most famous relations and rivalries with tennis.

The first major rival of Djokovic is Marat Safin. They first played each other on the final day of 2004's Miami Masters, with Safin beating Djokovic with straight sets. In the following year, the two met in the semifinals of Rome Masters, with Djokovic winning this time with a win in just three sets.

The most famous match between them was in 2005 at the Australian Open, where Safin beat Djokovic during the semifinals, winning with five sets. It was an enormous win for Safin and stopped Djokovic's streak of winning 26 times.

Djokovic got his revenge in the following year, but he would be defeated by Safin in the semi-finals in the Rogers Cup. The result was the start of a dynamite campaign for Djokovic who was able to take home every match between the two athletes.

His next biggest rival is Andy Murray. They first played each other in the second round at the 2006 Miami Masters, with Djokovic taking the title with ease in straight sets. The two would play again in the semi-finals at 2007's Wimbledon Championships, with Djokovic winning yet again the winner with straight sets.

It would mark the beginning of a run of winning four straight times for Djokovic against Murray and a win in the semi-finals of the Australian Open in 2008. Australian Open. In the end, Murray would finally get his first win against Djokovic in 2009 at the Madrid Masters, defeating him in the quarterfinals.

They would play again during the semifinals at the 2010 Australian Open, with Djokovic always coming out winning with straight sets. But, Murray would finally get his first win against Djokovic in 2009's Madrid Masters, defeating him in the quarterfinals.

They would play again during the semi-finals at The Australian Open in 2010. Australian Open, with Djokovic winning his second time with a win with straight sets.

The next major rival of Djokovic was Nadal. Nadal and Djokovic first faced off in the semi-finals at the 2005 French Open, with Nadal taking the title in just four sets. They'd meet again in the semis at the 2006 French Open, with Nadal winning the second time and coming out with a win with straight sets.

Nadal was also able to win their subsequent match that took place in the semifinals of 2007 Wimbledon Championships. But, Djokovic would finally get his first win against Nadal in the 2009 Miami Masters, defeating him in the final.

The match would mark the beginning of a string of four straight victories for Djokovic against Nadal and he also won the semis of the 2009 Australian Open and the 2010 US Open. Nadal could finally claim revenge in 2011, the French Open, defeating Djokovic in the final.

Both would face off in the final match of the 2012 Wimbledon Championships, with Djokovic winning his second time the winner with straight sets.

The next major rival for Djokovic was Federer. They first played each other in the semi-finals at The 2006 Miami Masters, with Federer triumphing by straight sets. The two would play again during the final in the 2007 Wimbledon Championships, with Federer yet again winning the winner with straight sets.

But, Djokovic would finally get his first victory against Federer in the 2009 US Open, defeating him in the semis. The result would set off a string of four consecutive wins for Djokovic against Federer and include wins at the 2009 Australian Open, the 2010 US Open, and the 2011 Wimbledon Championships.

Federer will finally take revenge during his 2012 French Open, defeating Djokovic in the semis. They would play again in the final match of 2013's Wimbledon Championships, with Djokovic winning his second time to come out with a win with straight sets.

The next major rival of Djokovic would be Andy Murray. They first played each other during the semi-finals at the 2006 Miami Masters, with Djokovic beating Murray by straight-sets. They'd meet again in the semi-finals in 2007's Wimbledon

Championships, with Djokovic winning yet again the winner with straight sets.

The start of the streak of four consecutive wins for Djokovic against Murray with a triumph in the semi-finals of the Australian Open in 2008. Australian Open. But, Murray would finally get his first win against Djokovic during the 2009 Madrid Masters, defeating him in the quarterfinals.

They would play again in the semi-finals in the 2010 Australian Open, with Djokovic winning his second time winning with straight sets. But, Murray would finally get his first victory over Djokovic during the 2009 Madrid Masters, defeating him in the quarterfinals.

They would play again during the semi-finals in the upcoming 2010, Australian Open, with Djokovic winning his second time the winner with straight sets.

The next major rival of Djokovic was Nadal. They first played during the semifinals at the 2005 French Open, with Nadal beating Djokovic in four sets. The two would play once more in the semifinals in the finals of 2006's French Open, with Nadal winning the second time and coming out with a win with straight sets.

Nadal won the next match and it was in the semifinals of 2007 Wimbledon Championships. But, Djokovic would finally get his first victory over Nadal in the 2009 Miami Masters, defeating him in the final.

It would kick off a run of four consecutive wins for Djokovic against Nadal and he also won semifinals at the 2009 Australian Open and the 2010 US Open. Nadal could finally claim revenge during 2011, the French Open, defeating Djokovic in the final.

Both would face off during the finals of the 2012 Wimbledon Championships, with Djokovic yet again winning the winner with straight sets.

His next biggest rival was Federer. Federer and Djokovic first faced off during the semifinals at The 2006 Miami Masters, with Federer triumphing with ease. They'd meet again in the finals in the 2007 Wimbledon Championships, with Federer yet again winning the winner with straight sets.

In the end, Djokovic would finally get his first win against Federer in the 2009 US Open, defeating him in the semis. It would begin a run of winning four straight times for Djokovic against Federer and include wins at the 2009 Australian Open, the 2010 US Open, and the 2011 Wimbledon Championships.

Federer was finally able to get revenge during his 2012 French Open, defeating Djokovic in the semi-finals. Both would face off in the final match of 2013's Wimbledon Championships, with Djokovic yet again winning with a win with straight sets.

The development of Djokovic's relationship with other players on and off court.

When Djokovic first came onto the scene of professional tennis the world, he was thought of as a promising tennis star. Many of his fellow players noticed of his potential and talent however, there was a sense of rivalry among the players. Djokovic wanted to be the best, and quickly moved to the top of the list, winning his very first Grand Slam title at the Australian Open in 2008. Australian Open.

The win made Djokovic as a formidable opponent to Roger Federer and Rafael Nadal. Both legends of tennis had been dominating tennis for many years and Djokovic became an opponent to their power. The result was a rise in the competition between Djokovic as well as his rivals in both the court and on the courts.

Even though Djokovic was always an intense competitor but he also has developed friendships with several of his players. Djokovic is well-known for his good sportsmanship as well as being a great partner to his opponents. Djokovic is also often credited with giving tips and advice to the younger athletes, helping them enhance their performance.

The change in Djokovic's relationship with other tennis players has been a good one. The Serbian has been thought of as an up-and-coming talent to being a renowned figure in tennis. His rivalries and connections make up a large part of his accomplishment as a tennis player as well as as a human.

Jokovic's Sportsmanship and respect for tennis players.

His sportsmanship and respect for tennis players can be seen by the manner in which he conducts his self on and off of the court. He always shows respect to his adversaries, no matter if they are winning or losing. Also, he has had the reputation of encouraging players after an intense game. Djokovic is also famous for his fairness and good sportsmanship. He's never been involved in any controversy on the court and always showed his respect for tennis. The relationships between Djokovic and his rivals on the tennis court are also testimony to his sporting character and respect. He's always maintained an excellent relationship with teammates, and even adversaries. He always showed them respect, and has not been associated in any controversy off court in any way. Djokovic is a genuine tennis player and is a fantastic role model for his sport of tennis.

The effect of rivalries on the career of Djokovic and his role in the history of tennis.

Rivalries have played an important part in the career of Djokovic, they have shaped his position in the history of tennis. They've provided tremendous motivators for him, spurring Djokovic to achieve new heights of achievement.

The first time Djokovic had a major battle was Roger Federer. They played each other at a series of highly-anticipated games, which included the Wimbledon finals in the year 2014. Djokovic won the contest, which established his position among the top athletes in the world. The competition of Djokovic and Federer has helped raise the image of tennis as well as enticed new fans into the game.

The rivalry between Djokovic and Rafael Nadal is also well-documented. Both players have played during several unforgettable matches of tennis, such as the Wimbledon final of the year 2011. Djokovic has been a huge results over Nadal and has won 14 of their 27 encounters. The squabble of Djokovic Nadal and Nadal has helped popularize tennis across the globe, and made tennis one of the most well-known sports.

His most recent match has been with Andy Murray. Murray and Djokovic have played in several important matches, such as the Wimbledon finals in 2013. Djokovic has been a huge victory over Murray with 12 wins in their 18 encounters. Their rivalry Djokovic Murray and Murray has contributed to the popularity of tennis throughout the world as well as helped turn it into among the top viewed games.

The rivalries between Djokovic have helped determine his place in the tennis world. These rivalries have also served as an incredible source of motivation for Djokovic in pushing him to achieve the next level of his success.

Chapter 8: Family and Personal Journey

Personal life of Djokovic, which includes his family and marriage.

His personal life is relatively quiet in comparison to his professional. He got married to his long-time partner, Jelena Ristic, in the year 2014. The couple has two children in their lives, a son called Stefan and an infant daughter called Tara. Djokovic is a man of the family and cherishes time with his children and wife. The Serbian tennis player has stated that family is his top prioritization, over the sport of tennis. Djokovic can also be described as a charitable person and is the founder of his own foundation, the Novak Djokovic Foundation, which offers support for children living in Serbia. In the year 2020, Djokovic was awarded the Laureus World Sportsman of the Award. This award is awarded to an athlete who "demonstrated the greatest sporting achievement of the year." Djokovic was the first tennis player to receive this award since it was first introduced at the age of 2000.

Djokovic He balances professional tennis and the demands of a family.

in 2009 Djokovic got married to his former lover, Jelena Ristic. They have two kids with each other: a son named Stefan who was born in 2014 and an infant daughter named Tara which was born in 2021.

Djokovic has been vocal about the importance of his family for him, and also how he is able to manage his career in tennis with his obligations to his family. He's said it is a blessing to be surrounded by a loving wife and kids who appreciate his passion for tennis.

Djokovic has stated that he strives to be at home as often as he can during his time at home. He also said is determined that he spends time with his family whenever it is possible. Additionally, he tries to stay on top of the activities and schooling of his kids.

Djokovic has talked about the way his family been a huge help in keeping him in the right place and that they are the biggest supporter. He's said the way he has achieved all the things he has achieved without their support and love.

The cultural roots of Djokovic and their impact on his career as well as his identity.

The Djokovic's culture and heritage as well as its impact on his professional career as well as his identity are a fascinating narrative. Djokovic is a native of Serbia and his family has Montenegrin heritage. The father of Djokovic, Srdjan was a former professional footballer and their mother, Dijana, is a household worker. The elder brother of Djokovic, Marko, is also a tennis professional. His family is close to and have been in support of his tennis career.

The cultural background of Djokovic has been a key factor in shaping his character. He's extremely satisfied with his Montenegrin origins, and often talks about the ways his heritage influences his work. Djokovic claims that his Montenegrin culture has taught him a strong drive to succeed and an unstoppable attitude. These traits have enabled him to be one of the top tennis players on the planet.

His cultural roots have also affected his play style. The Serbian is well-known for his ferocious and powerful style of tennis that is frequently compared with that of his countryman Novak Djokovic. The rich cultural roots of Djokovic have also allowed him to connect with his players from around the globe. The Serbian is well-known for his warm and outgoing manner of speaking, and frequently spends time with fans, and even make autographs.

His cultural background is an integral aspect of his life story which is a major influence on his life and career. Djokovic is proud Montenegrin and his cultural heritage has helped shape him into the accomplished tennis player and individual that he is now.

Hobbies and interests of Djokovic other than tennis.

His interests and passions beyond tennis are numerous and diverse. He's a voracious reader and his most-loved novel is "The Catcher in the Rye." Also, he enjoys playing piano and his top composition includes "Rhapsody in Blue." Animals are his passion, and has a favorite pet, the dog Pierre. Additionally, he's a major fan of the film "The Godfather." In his free time,

Djokovic enjoys spending time with his friends and family.

The lessons learned from personal experience and the impact they have on the mindset of Djokovic.

In his autobiography Djokovic talks about his personal experience and the way they affected his mental outlook. One of these was the battle with depression. Djokovic was afflicted with depression for years however, it was only when the time he sought help from a professional that he could beat the condition. This incident was a lesson for Djokovic how important it was to seek aid when confronted with problems in your life. This also taught him how important it is to keep positive attitude towards life even when times seem difficult.

Another thing that made a significant impact on Djokovic was his transition to becoming a dad. Djokovic along with his wife Jelena was the first to welcome their baby, Stefan, in 2014. The birth of Stefan transformed Djokovic in numerous ways. He was more patient and understanding. He was also able to control his time and energy. Being a parent also led to Djokovic more conscious of how important family is. Djokovic realized that his family was the most significant factor in his life and has put in efforts to spend longer with them in recent times.

Personal experiences like these have had a an impact on the tennis player's attitude. Djokovic has benefited from his experiences and has grown into a better person for it. Djokovic is aware of his mental state, and is now more willing to seek help in the event of need. Also, he's conscious of his family members and spending quality time with his family. This has created Djokovic a more confident person in both the mental and emotional aspects.

Chapter 9: Legacy and Impact on the Sport

His impact on the game of tennis, as well as its international recognition.

The moment that Djokovic came onto the scene in the mid 2000s tennis was in dire need of a fresh superstar. It was dominated by Roger Federer and Rafael Nadal for over a decade and even though both are famous players in the sport however, their dominance has led to tennis becoming dull. Djokovic transformed everything.

The Serbian brought a new degree of athleticism and style to tennis. his battle between Nadal and Federer brought back enthusiasm for tennis across the globe. Djokovic also had the unbeatable talent to attract people of all ages and his popularity helped expand the game across new areas.

Tennis is now becoming more well-known than it ever was and Djokovic is the primary reason for this. He has influenced a younger generation of players and followers, and his influence on tennis is going to be felt for a number of years to be. Much of the credit goes to Djokovic tennis is now back to be one of the most loved sports around the world.

Examining the place Djokovic has in tennis legends.

In the world of tennis it is clear that Djokovic is considered to be one of the great players of all time. His status among the legends in tennis is confirmed through his numerous achievements, in and out of the court. Djokovic has been awarded several Grand Slam titles, including the record-breaking seven Australian Open titles. Also, he has held the world's No. number one ranking for a span of 302 weeks. This is third in ever. Alongside his numerous achievements, Djokovic is also known for his charity work and dedication to giving his back to the game of tennis. He founded his own foundation, the Novak Djokovic Foundation, which offers assistance to children who are not well-off in Serbia. Additionally, he has donated funds to other charitable organizations which include those affected by the 2020 bush fires in Australia. The impact of Djokovic on the game of tennis is evident. He has encouraged a whole younger generation of tennis players, and has contributed to the growth of the game in his homeland of Serbia. He's a tennis icon and will be remembered as one of the best tennis players ever.

Record-breaking achievements, awards and milestones achievable through Djokovic throughout his professional career.

Novak Djokovic is one of the tennis stars with the highest success in history. He has won many titles and was ranked as no. #1 in the world numerous times. He also has achieved numerous records and landmarks in his life.

The most memorable achievements are his winning of his first Wimbledon singles crown in the year 2011 and becoming the first Serbian player to take home an official Grand Slam singles title. In addition, he has won his Australian Open singles title six times, winning the title for four consecutive times from 2015 until the year 2018. The only eight males to win all nine tournaments of the ATP Masters 1000 tournaments. Djokovic is also a winner of Olympic gold medals in doubles, singles and mixed doubles.

Djokovic has set numerous other records and achievements throughout his playing career. He is the sole tennis player to win all four Grand Slam junior titles, the ATP Masters 1000 tournaments, and also an Olympic gold medal. Also, he is the only tennis player to win all nine ATP Masters 1000 tournaments. Djokovic has taken home the total of an astounding 82 ATP singles titles. This is third in all-time wins. In addition, he has held a record of thirty ATP Masters 1000 titles.

Djokovic's achievements and record-breaking performances are evidence of his talents and dedication. He's had an immense influence on the game of tennis, and has encouraged other tennis players to strive higher to achieve their goals. The legacy of Djokovic will guide future generations of tennis players and their fans alike.

Influence of Djokovic's has a profound effect on the next generations of tennis stars.

In the year that Novak Djokovic won his maiden French Open title in 2016 this was a record-setting Grand Slam and cemented his status in the pantheon of top tennis players ever. The greatest impact of Djokovic's win in the game could be yet to come.

The success of Djokovic on the court has provided motivation to the next class of tennis pros. He has demonstrated that you can excel in tennis even without the characteristics of a serve-and-volley athlete or a baseline slacker. His all-court game has become an example for the future generation of tennis players.

His impact on the game is being noticed off the court. He is an active supporter of the rights of players and was a major driving factor in the creation of the ATP Player Council. Djokovic utilizes his position to help make game better for everyone, both present and in the future.

The new generation of tennis stars will be affected by Djokovic in various ways. Djokovic is an example in and off court and his influence on tennis will continue to be felt for many years to follow.

The long-lasting legacy and contribution of Djokovic for the sport.

The legacy of Djokovic and his contributions to tennis are numerous and long-lasting. He's been a major player in tennis for over a decade having won many Grand Slam titles and setting many records. He's also been an innovator in the game and has helped to promote the usage of backhands with two hands and serve-and-volley.

His impact on tennis has been significant. He has contributed to raising the playing level and inspired many younger tennis players to chase their goals of being professionals in tennis. His contributions and achievements to the game will be remembered for the many years to come.

Chapter 10: Business Ventures and Endorsements

The business and entrepreneurial ventures of Djokovic as well as his initiatives.

Djokovic's entrepreneurial and business ventures are numerous and diverse. The year 2006 was the time he established his own tennis academy named the Novak Djokovic Academy, in his home town of Belgrade, Serbia. It is a cutting-edge establishment that provides tennis training and instruction for students from around the globe. Alongside being a part of the school, Djokovic has a luxurious clothing line as well as a range of nutritional supplements, as well as numerous eateries.

The clothing line of Novak Djokovic, dubbed "Serbia by Novak Djokovic" is a premium range of casual clothes which is available in high-end department stores and on the internet. The collection includes men's as well as women's apparel in addition to children's clothes. The line of nutritional supplements from Djokovic known as "Nuvo", is sold at health food stores as well as on-line. Nuvo is a line that includes a wide range of items, such as vitamin powder, protein powder as well as energy bars.

Restaurants owned by Djokovic are "Novak", a fine dining establishment in Belgrade as well as "Djokovic's", a more informal restaurant located in Dubai. Djokovic also holds an ownership stake of the Serbian coffee firm named "Moka Coffee". Apart from his commercial initiatives, Djokovic is also an active donor to charities. He founded his foundation, the Novak Djokovic Foundation, which gives financial support and help for children living in Serbia living in poor conditions.

An analysis of Djokovic's endorsements, as well as branding collaborations.

In the year 2011, Djokovic signed a four-year 40 million dollar deal with Japanese clothing company UNIQLO that was the biggest endorsement contract ever done by a tennis player in the era of. Other endorsement agreements signed by Djokovic include Adidas, Head, Seiko and Peugeot. All in all, Djokovic has earned over 200 million dollars in endorsement contracts during his professional career.

The biggest partnership for Djokovic's brand is UNIQLO the company he partnered with in the year 2011. The four-year deal, worth $40 million over the course of four years was one of the highest-paying endorsement contract ever done by a tennis player at the time. Djokovic claims that the reason he signed with UNIQLO due to the company's dedication to innovation and quality.

Djokovic is also claiming that he feels connected to UNIQLO due to the company's Japanese origins.

Other endorsements signed by Djokovic comprise Adidas, Head, Seiko as well as Peugeot. All in all, Djokovic has earned over 200 million dollars from endorsements throughout his playing career.

The endorsements of Djokovic have allowed the development of a global image. Djokovic has stated that it is his intention to make use of his platform to spread the message of healthful living as well as to encourage other people to chase their goals. Djokovic has stated that he would like to utilize his name to support the businesses of his homeland Serbia.

His philanthropy as well as commercial ventures.

The philanthropic and commercial endeavors of Djokovic include a variety of philanthropic ventures and are numerous. Apart from his involvement in Novak Djokovic Foundation, a charity Novak Djokovic Foundation, which helps children from Serbia and beyond, he's created a range of companies and merchandise. The businesses include a tennis school as well as a line of nutrition-based products, as well as clothing lines. In addition, he has been a sought-after endorsement partnership who lends his brand and name to brands such as Adidas, Head, and Uniqlo.

His work through his foundation has aided in improving life for children from Serbia. The foundation grants financial aid to those in need in addition to funding for education programs as well as extracurricular activities. Djokovic also uses his platform to increase awareness of how important education is. He has been an active proponent of the rights of children.

The businesses of Djokovic have proven to be successful as his products have been widely appreciated by customers. His tennis school is considered to be among the top around the globe, and his nutrition products have received praise for their effectiveness and quality. The clothing collection has been a hit, as have his endorsement contracts have proven very profitable.

His philanthropic efforts and ventures in commercial business has made him among the most accomplished athletes around the globe. The Serbian athlete is a source of inspiration for youngsters and is an example for business. His activities have contributed to enhance life of kids living in Serbia and helped make him an affluent man.

The business aspect of the career of Djokovic and his branding management.

Novak Djokovic's professional career in tennis has been nothing short extraordinary. He has been awarded numerous Grand Slam titles and is in the midst of being ranked as the top player on the planet. 1 player. The success of Djokovic's extends beyond his tennis successes. Djokovic has also proven adept in the business aspect of his professional career. He has created a formidable image.

Djokovic has several endorsement agreements with the most famous brands around the world, such as Adidas, Lacoste, and UNIQLO. The deals helped him make tens of millions of dollars annually. Alongside the endorsements he has signed, Djokovic has also launched numerous successful businesses. His own brand of tennis clothing with UNIQLO as well as a line of nutritional supplements known as Novak Nutrition, and a tennis academy in his homeland of Serbia.

His success both in court and off has helped him become one of the top sportspersons worldwide. The number of followers on his social media is a huge one and he's utilized his platform to market his companies and endorsers. Djokovic is also involved in charitable giving and has given thousands of dollars numerous charitable organizations.

Overall, Djokovic has built an amazing career as well as a image. He's an experienced businessman, and has made use of his fame to market his endorsements and businesses. Djokovic is an incredibly generous donor and is using his fame to aid other individuals.

The balancing act between Djokovic's tennis prowess and his business endeavors.

For the last 10 years, Djokovic has been one of the top tennis players on the planet. He has been awarded numerous Grand Slam titles and has been ranked at No. one worldwide for a number of years.

But, Djokovic is not just an excellent tennis player. Djokovic is also a thriving businessman. There are a variety of partnerships and ventures in business which have helped him become one of the most successful tennis players around the globe.

Djokovic was always attracted to business. He founded a tennis school in his home country of Serbia as well as made investments in different businesses. These ventures in business have proven extremely successful and have earned an enormous amount of money.

However, the business activities of Djokovic are not always easy. There has been criticism of him from those who believe Djokovic is more focused on earning money rather than the winning of tennis games.

Djokovic has maintained for years that he's determined to focus on his career in tennis and business projects. The Serbian has stated that he would like to achieve success both in his life.

The business ventures of Djokovic have enabled him to enjoy a well-off life. He owns a lavish home in Monaco as well as several properties across the globe.

The business ventures of Djokovic have brought him plenty of liberty. The Serbian can go anywhere he likes and not need to think about the cost of his travels.

His business ventures with Djokovic have been highly profitable. He has however, always stated that his primary goal is tennis. He hopes to be known for being one of the most renowned tennis players of all time.

Chapter 11: The Evolution Continues

His ongoing professional career continues and his desire to continue his achievements.

Novak Djokovic has been one of the top tennis players over the past decade. He has won several Grand Slam titles and is at the moment ranked the No. #1 on the planet. The career of Djokovic has been defined by constant excellence, as well as a desire to constantly increase.

The desire of Djokovic to make his next achievements is evident during the past few time. There have been significant adjustments in his play, such as changing to a different racket as well as hiring a brand new coach. These adjustments have enabled Djokovic to be much more effective, such as in his win at Wimbledon as well as in the US Open in 2018.

The desire of Djokovic to continue improving and advancing his technique is certain to be a constant over the next few years. The tennis player's passion and commitment to his sport are apparent, and it's evident that Djokovic is determined to continue winning at the top level. With many more years in the sport ahead, Djokovic looks poised to bring many wins as well as achievements to his amazing professional career.

Reviewing the recent performance of Djokovic and adjusting to new challenges.

In the last few years, Djokovic has made some important adjustments in his play. He's increased the topspin of his backhand and forehand and has enhanced the velocity of his serve. These adjustments have enabled him to be more consistent and helped him be in control of his shot. However, these changes have led to him being more vulnerable for attackers.

In the most recent of his tournaments, Djokovic lost to an uncompromising opponent in the semis. It has caused to him to review his strategy and implement some adjustments. Djokovic is trying to add the power of his shots as well as being more aggressive in his own play. Additionally, he's striving to improve his footwork, so it is easier to defend himself against attackers.

The changes made by Djokovic show that his willingness to change to the new demands. He's always evolving as a player, and is constantly looking to make improvements. That's why Djokovic an amongst the most successful athletes in the world.

Djokovic's search for more Grand Slam titles and records.

The year 2012 was a great one for Djokovic. Djokovic achieved a record-setting year, winning 3 Grand Slam singles titles and becoming the first person ever since Rod Laver in 1969 to have all four Grand Slam titles in the same year. Also, he set the record for longest consecutive weeks in no. 1. in the ATP rankings. His success in the ATP rankings this season was due in large part due to his psychological game. The Serbian had been working with an expert in sports psychology to aid him in conquering the habit of choking during large matches. The outcomes were apparent. Djokovic seemed more calm and confident in court, which was apparent through his performance.

The following decades, Djokovic continued to rack the Grand Slam titles and break records. He clinched a record-breaking 7th Australian Open title in 2020 He also became the first person during the Open Era to win all 9 of the Masters 1000 tournaments. His quest to earn more Grand Slam titles and records will continue to grow in the coming years. Djokovic is currently ranked no. one in the world and, at only 32 He has many years of achievement ahead of him.

The impact of the career of Djokovic in the tennis world's future.

In the year that Novak Djokovic first hit the tennis court, he was an unassuming teenager who had plenty of potential. In the course of time the player has become one of the best tennis players in history. His influence on tennis is immense, and the tennis future is looking very bright because of his efforts.

Djokovic is always an exceptional player, however his real brilliance has resulted from hard work and commitment. He's been working hard to make his game better and this has definitely resulted in a positive outcome. He's one of the best gamers in the world and has shown no signs of getting any slower.

His impact on the next generation of tennis is double-sided. In the first place, he has inspired the next generation of tennis players to be adamant and never stop pursuing their ambitions. Additionally, he's raising the playing level overall. In the event that he continues to dominate his sport, the other players will have to improve their game in order to be competitive with him.

The future of tennis is promising, and the majority of it is because of Novak Djokovic. Novak Djokovic is a phenomenal player that has transformed the game in a positive way. Because of him this generation of athletes is going to be better than the one before them.

A look back at Djokovic's career and contribution to the game.

Djokovic's rise to reach the heights of the world tennis scene is one of the most remarkable. He was born in a tiny city in Serbia and has worked to rise through the ranks until he became one of the top tennis players around the globe. The journey he has taken on has been an inspiration for many, and his impact on the sport has been enormous.

Djokovic was always a gifted player. However, it is his dedication and commitment that turned him the world-class player he is currently. He's always willing to work more hours in the court and resulted in him winning. His climb to the top is an incredible one. His contribution to the game has been huge.

Chapter 12: Novak tennis and Serbia

Novak Djokovic could survive the conflict; he would become the first member of his family to own the tennis racquet, and the tennis champion would be able to defeat Nadal Federer and Nadal, but prior to that, he was born in Belgrade, Serbia, on May 22nd the 22nd of May, 1987.

Srdjan Djokovic was Novak's dad. Fans of sports all over the world recognize him as the man with sunglasses, wearing a t-shirt featuring Novak's image. In the past the time, he was a skiing instructor as well as working in the business of sports equipment. Srdjan saw Novak's mother Dijana at a slope. Novak is the eldest of the three brothers from the Djokovic family. Marko Djokovic was born in 1991. Djordje Djokovic was born the year 1995. Both played alongside Novak into the tennis court.

The family of Novak was extremely athletic, and they played in a variety of different sports. The two most popular were soccer and skiing. most popular sports, and so Novak being a tennis player was a pleasant surprise. The fact that there were tennis courts constructed at the Kopaonik ski resort in the area where the family owned a business that was a success, came as a surprise. Tennis was his first sport when he was the age of four. Because they were impressed by his abilities the family backed to him in all ways by granting loans for his coaching, and he was disciplined. When he later moved into a tennis club and was disciplined, his performance and determination shocked the coaches because Novak did not just take each and every session with seriousness and would show on time to get ready for practice sessions.

Jelena Gencic had stumbled upon Monica Seles, and at the tennis camps she saw that Novak was the star in the near future. He was her coach, and she knew Novak was not just gifted and athletic, but at 6 or seven was well-prepared to make a career in professional tennis; as well, Novak stated to her that the goal of his was: "No. one player on the planet!" Tennis was Novak's his future. He played in a few ski races in his early years.

Srdjan understood the way he was acting as the man who pushed Novak to help him realize the potential of tennis "Only Novak mattered. Everyone else, including his family members and coaches, weren't important. Every effort was made to help Novak succeed in what he's done in the present. When I noticed something that was not working in the way I had planned, I'd change places, and find an additional coach."

His job as a parent was a big part of his day, however it was a great location to work in an eatery serving pizza located in a mountain lodge. The restaurant would offer pizza and pancakes. He also worked out by removing the snow for customers to walk into. If it was raining or snowing, Djokovic was playing tennis in the rain, and also used Pete Sampras as someone to emulate his play.

At the time he was born the nation was Yugoslavia And wars could result in the nation dissolving. The wars would continue in Serbia as well as Montenegro. Novak must be vigilant for aerial assaults, yet he was still able to practice tennis. One method that he and his instructor used included playing tennis at the spot where the attack occurred because it wasn't logical for the area to be attacked with bombs again.

Much of his time in Serbia was spent in the Serbian Orthodox Church. The church taught him not just about his religion, but in addition, about helping other people and in the future, he was active in numerous charitable causes. In 2011, the Catholic Church awarded the highest honour to Novak who was awarded the Order from St. Sava of the First Degree. The tennis community has been noticing that Novak has the wooden cross. It was acquired at Hilandar which is a monastic community situated on the top of a mountain in Greece. Novak was there from 2009, saying "The most we did was to pray throughout the day long, go for walks doing some chores as well as eat every daily, between 6:30 a.m. as well as 6 p.m. It brings you back to your roots, and return to your self." Being a part of the Eastern Orthodox religion does have added benefits today. When he travels across the globe for tennis tournaments

Novak is greeted by not just Serbs but as well Greeks, Bulgarians and other those who adhere to Novak's Orthodox religion.

Novak was still a youngster however, he was outgrowing playing tennis in Serbia. He was just too talented and had a lot of potential in a nation which didn't have the top facilities or top coaches to help him develop his skills. The coach he had in Serbia declared that Novak was going to have to move somewhere else to be a superstar which is when Djokovic began his quest to become the most successful tennis player of the the world.

Chapter 13: The German Tennis Academy

He was just twelve at the time his departure from Serbia to join an education at the Niki Pilic Academy near Munich in 1999. Pilic was awestruck: "I soon realized after an hour of playing with his character that he was a man with an amazing determination. He was a great coach due to the fact that he had what was required to reach the areas which no coach could penetrate, such as the brain and heart." At first, when he was approached by Gencic Pilic believed the young Novak is too old to be a coach and he was not convinced. However, the coach soon made a decision to go along Novak as well as Goran his Uncle Goran headed to Germany.

Pilic was a tennis player who had an impressive coach and playing career in tennis. Pilic had taught Goran Ivanisevic as well as Michael Stich at his academy. Novak will surpass what the two legendary players achieved, but in the moment the time, he was just a teenager who was learning about how to play. This was a difficult time for his mom, whom she was deeply saddened by particularly during his first year of absence. Also, it was very expensive and the Djokovic family was required to pay some thousand dollars each month to cover Novak's stay at the academy and travel expenses to competitions. At the end of the day, it certainly was worth the work his parents put into. In the courtroom, no one put in as much effort than the young Novak.

Novak developed a game approach that eventually would have none weaknesses. This was a style where he believed that every shot was an opportunity to earn the ball, and he became the best returner around the globe. And even if he failed to hit the shot that won and his lengthy rallies lead to his opponent making the wrong shot. The right-handed shot he played resulted in shots with high speed and his double-handed backhand could be a weapon that only a handful of players were able to match.

Novak earned the nickname "Nole." It was simply a shorter version of the name. It was one less letter, but it halved the amount of the syllables. Djokovic proved to be efficient and successful not just on the court, as well as when deciding on his nickname. In the future, tennis and media gave him many different names. The Joker would become The Serbinator, Djoker, Djoko, Nox and The Joker. Later, in the past If Federer or Nadal were heroes to tennis enthusiasts, just as in the case of Batman and Robin There was a requirement of The Djoker to take on the two.

The Serbian had some success Novak when he competed at tournaments both for himself as well as for Serbia. The most notable win was in singles for 14 and under category of the European Junior Championships. Djokovic was a wise man beyond age, and when was contemplating what his needs would be in the future, he was able to surprise his coaches when they asked them to instruct him in English. Novak became proficient in five languages. Pilic might have rearranged Novak's stance on the racquet However, Novak relied on him and others to improve more than tennis. Along with his parents, Novak has given credit to many of his coaches including Gencic and Pilic in the past, as well as Marian Vajda and Boris Becker. The other coaches of Novak have been Dejan Petrovic, Riccardo Piatti, Mark Woodforde and Todd Martin.

Goran Ivanisevic was a tennis player together with Novak during 2000. Goran had heard that Djokovic was the future of tennis and after he played on the opposite end of the net with Novak for some time, Goran started to think the assessment was accurate. As of 2001 Novak won the doubles as well as singles titles of the European Juniors. There were few who worked as hard like Novak and he was training all day long and dedicate his entire life to tennis. Djokovic was able to grow up to 6'2 inches tall And as he gained weight and became more proficient He began to participate in Futures competitions to take a move towards becoming a player on the World Tour.

In 2003, Novak met Jelena Ristic. They began dating two years after. They and their dog, Pierre, would attend numerous tennis tournaments over the course of the 10 years. Novak and Jelena were set to marry in 2014.

In the courtroom, Novak didn't take long to see the right path to victory during

2003. Novak also saw rapid improvements. He first lost straight-sets in the Futures Event in Munich. Then he lost the subsequent event in Serbia and he took one set of Manuel Jorquera. Novak was able to relax knowing that he would be returning to Serbia in his subsequent event in June 2003. He could use this, along with his excellent tennis skills to take the title. Novak was awarded $118 in the two previous events, however, he was awarded $1,300 in this major victory. Djokovic was also awarded the tennis rank 768 on the planet.

The year ended with three events remaining in Serbia in the Futures circuit. The first ended in a defeat in the first round but he was able to make it to the semifinals at the two other events. Nole was in 2004 when he competed in an Challenger tournament in Serbia. The event ended in defeat for the first round.

Novak played in several ITF Futures events and kept growing his skills and improving his world rankings. Hungary was a good place to test Novak He won the Futures event at Szolnok. The debut ATP Challenger Tour tournament win occurred just prior to his debut every World Tour event. In the month of May, 2004, Novak was ranked at 515 worldwide and defeated five players that were higher ranked to take the title held in Budapest, Hungary.

Novak Djokovic was beating older players at junior tournaments, and also extremely competitive against top players at the men's level. It was the right time for Novak to move up to the very top level of the sport. Novak was ranked 368 worldwide.

Chapter 14: 2005 Australian Open Qualifier

It is believed that the ATP World Tour professional career of Djokovic began in 2004, after he was able to qualify for the Umag competition in Croatia. It was a tight match in the initial set but the expertise of Italian tennis player Filippo Volandri proved too to handle for the young Novak losing 7-6 6-1. Novak was beaten in the majority of aspects of the match which was played on clay. However, he produced four aces with none of his rivals. This was not a good beginning to his professional career at the top of his game however it was a good starting point. Also, it was the start of major tournaments and when Djokovic lost during the opening round of Umag and he earned an extra amount of money from it than taking home his place in the Challenger Tour tournament in Hungary a few months prior.

In the following month, August, he went down to Futures level, however the player also improved his level with a win at a tournament held in Serbia. He was a swath of success at the event that was small held in Belgrade, Serbia. In the final, Novak beat Flavio Cipolla 6-4, 7-6. Novak followed up with Challenger Tour events in Italy and Germany with 2 match wins in the two events, and then back in the bigger and more impressive ATP World Tour event.

The first time he won the ATP World Tour event match was against Arnaud Clement in the Romanian Open in Bucharest. The serve, and particularly his second serve that helped propel Djokovic into victory. The Serbian couldn't beat David Ferrer in the next round. David Ferrer was the Spaniard was a decade older than Djokovic and was ranked at more than 200 spots more than him at the time. The situation would alter as time went on. Although Ferrer could get four more victories against Novak however, it would be Djokovic that would take the lead. In 2012, Djokovic could have nine victories over Ferrer.

On the next list of priorities to be next on the list for Djokovic when he was learning how to be among the best players in the world was travel. Although he was playing across Europe and continental Europe but he was yet to go on tour around all over the world in the ATP World Tour. It was his first taste of it in the month of September, as he traveled to Thailand. Nole traveled all his way into Bangkok, Thailand, to be defeated by one who was from Holland. Dennis van Scheppingen defeated Djokovic in three sets. This was only a minor setback; Novak returned to Europe In November, he took the title at the

Challenger competition at Aachen, Germany.

In the world rankings, which was within 200, for the very first time in his career, Novak completed the year with two additional Challenger races. In Slovakia the country he was competing in, he came across the hero of his home town Dominik Hrbaty in the 2nd round, but lost. Hrbaty was in the 14th position at the time. Novak's 2004 campaign ended in Finland and he was eliminated during the 2nd round of the tournament to the Japanese Takao Suzuki. The year was a success for Novak. year that included the Davis Cup match against Latvia however, he was also thinking about more important things in mind including an eventual Grand Slam appearance.

At the beginning of in 2005 Novak had qualified to earn a spot at his first appearance at the Australian Open, and his prize was a match against the huge Russian Marat Safin. He was on best of his game at that time. He was ranked at 4 and Safin was a 6-0 winner 7-1, 6-2, and 6-1. What Djokovic did not know was that he'd already defeated by the man that would ultimately win the match. Novak gained experience, he was able to experience the atmosphere during the largest of tennis competitions, the Grand Slam; and as the prize available for the tournament was $6743,444, this was a good cash prize despite losing the tennis match quickly.

In the era of tennis the four best athletes included Roger Federer, Andy Roddick and Lleyton Hewitt. Safin. Safin defeated Hewitt at the Australian Open final in four sets. Andre Agassi was also still active in tennis. Marcos Baghdatis was a qualifier similar to Novak however, he made it to the 16th round prior to losing against Federer; Nadal was an unseeded tennis player. Gael Monfils, a wild card entry. Novak returned to Melbourne, Australia, many times. Melbourne was the place where he scored the most memorable victories, as well as some hard moments.

At 177, he was ranked the highest, Djokovic returned to Serbia to play in an Challenger Tour event in February. He took two wins and then lost in the final to Dick Norman. In the wake of two smaller tournaments and a return to the ATP World Tour event in Spain and lost in the opening round. Then he won in a Challenger event at San Remo, and next was a Grand Slam appearance, at the French Open. As with many other players, clay wasn't an area of strength for him at the beginning of his career however, it was on clay that Novak won his first game during an actual Grand Slam. Novak beat Robby Ginepri in a 6-0, 6-0 7-3 despite the fact that Ginepri was more highly in the world, at 71%, while Novak was 53. Novak lost the second round against Guillermo Coria after retiring in the third set.

The remainder of the year saw Novak participating in a variety of major competitions, however the most important was the remaining two Grand Slams. The improvement he showed continued throughout the year. In January in the year, he had qualified to compete in his very first Grand Slam; at the French Open, he won his first ever match at an Grand Slam; and at Wimbledon and the US Open, he won the first two games at every event. Sebastien Grosjean knocked him out of Wimbledon. The US Open, Djokovic defeated Gael Monfils, and later Mario Ancic before losing to Fernando Verdasco in five sets.

At the beginning of 2006, Novak was ranked inside the top 100. she was preparing to head south to play in at the

Australian Open. The first round was a second loss against Paul Goldstein. He was a little lower in the rankings of the world, but by only five positions. The improvement was evident during his next tournament which was an event in the World Tour tournament in Zagreb with three victories before falling to the highly ranked Ivan Ljubicic. Then he defeated Tim Henman in a match at Rotterdam. Following a couple of events, he'd do something important on April 1st in the ATP World Tour Masters in Monte Carlo. The match was Novak in the final against Roger.

Roger Federer was top of the world ranking at that time. He had become a professional player in 1998 and was older that Djokovic was. As the match began, it was a bit tense in the first set, and Novak wasn't completely out of in his. Federer was able to win one set in the first game, but Novak took the second but Federer getting the final. Future rivalries began the next day. It was 6-3, 2-6 3-3. Federer defeated Novak later on in 2006, during the Davis Cup event.

As he continued to climb upwards in the rankings, Djokovic continued to show the tennis community that he is strong, and in the French Open, he made a huge announcement. He faced four players and then faced the world's number. 2 Rafael Nadal in a quarter-final match. Novak fell in two sets in a row, losing 6-4, and 6-4. He then ended his match. Wimbledon was the same: Novak won his first three games, but lost to the world's No. 10 Mario Ancic. Novak was at the top of the world rankings and many believed it wouldn't not be too long before he took home an event. Novak won his very first ATP World Tour title the following month.

Players of tennis have frequently changed nations throughout their career, at this time in his professional career, Novak was approached for a opportunity to represent Great Britain. In the moment, he stated, "It's just rumors. People were extremely kind towards us following winning the Davis Cup. We talked to them. There was nothing serious about it, actually. The two of us didn't engage in any seriously argued discussion regarding an identity card." The tennis in England received a greater amount of support than Novak was receiving in Serbia However, Djokovic realized that he earned enough money to stay with his career; although there were plenty of reasons for him to relocate but he was content with his Serbian player.

Chapter 15: First ATP Title

Few athletes are able to claim that they took home a trophy but afterwards, they also purchased it. But that's the case with

Djokovic was able to do. It took several years and a wealth of cash prizes between his initial title and the purchase of the tournament. But it happened.

His first win in his professional career playing on the ATP World Tour was the Dutch Open at Amersfoort, Netherlands. Novak did not face a lot of trouble either, he was able to win without losing one set. The tournament in July of 2006 had him beating Serbian Boris Pashanski, Tomas Zib, Marc Gicquel and Guillermo Coria to reach the final. First set against Nicolas Massu went to a tie-break. Novak took the lead and won the next set with a score of 6-4. Both were equally matched in the moment: Massu was ranked at 37 while Novak was ranked at 36. Together, they scored 20 aces during the game and Novak scoring nine Aces. Novak won his first major tournament win which was played with clay.

Novak was among the other notable participants in the tournament, including Rod Laver, John Newcombe, Guillermo Vilas and Thomas Muster. In the following years, Djokovic would buy the tournament and relocate the tournament to his country of birth and rename this tournament the Serbia Open. It was held with clay at Belgrade. Between 2009 and 2011, Novak won the championship.

Following his debut World Tour win, Novak was looking to win more awards. The chance to win one was almost during his subsequent event which was held in Umag, Croatia, but was forced to withdraw in the final match against Stan Wawrinka. Novak then lost during the 3rd round of the US Open, to Lleyton Hewitt. Afterwards, after defeating Federer and beating Stan Wawrinka in the Davis Cup Novak was able to claim the second time he won a World Tour event win. In

October 2006, he won in Metz. The event was held indoors. Novak completed the season with three additional tournaments. In one tournament, he was defeated by Wawrinka in Vienna however, in another event, he beat Andy Murray in Spain a few days later. Then, he focused on 2007 and seemed prepared for the start of 2007 with a win at the very first event he took part in.

The 16th-ranked player worldwide, Djokovic played in a warm-up competition in Australia before his participation in the Open held in Melbourne. He beat five of his opponents in the final to take home the crown in Adelaide. The tournament was the perfect way to prepare ahead of Australian Open. Australian Open, and it brought Novak up to 15th on the list of top players in the world. Federer as well as Nadal were seeded at numbers 1 2 and 1. Novak was seeded at 14 and Andy Murray seeded at 15. Marat Safin was seeded as the 26th seed.

2007. The Australian Open started very well for Novak who won an easy 6-1, 6-0 winning 6-0 against Massu. Feliciano Lopez lost at the end of the round by straight sets. Then, following Djokovic defeated Danai Udomchoke in the Round of 16, it was Djokovic against Federer in the round of 16. This was an example where the former champion was just superior to the youngest tennis player. Federer defeated Djokovic 6-2, 7-5 (7-5, 6-3). Federer was able to win the majority of his first-serve points, and also gave Novak only a handful of break point chances. In this moment, Federer was too good.

After two ATP competitions across Europe, Novak headed off for Dubai. He was victorious in his first two games, but the Swiss Superman came back to block his path. Novak has improved and won two of five break points that during the game. Also, he won the set. But it was not enough. Roger took the match 6-3, 7-6 or 3-3. It was going to take several months until Federer returned to the court from Novak as well, and in the next few months, he would play many encounters against the other nemesis of Federer, Nadal.

In the month of March 2007 Novak took part in 2 ATP Masters Series events in the USA And he performed extremely good. At both tournaments, he was up against Nadal and Murray and also David Ferrer and Evgeny Korolev. In the Indian Wells tournament, Novak came in with a ranking of 13and was able to climb up to 10 after reaching the final. Novak beat Andy Murray to get to the final but fell the title to Nadal in a match of 7-5, 6-2. Then, a few weeks later it was changed to Florida following Djokovic defeated Nadal in a match of 6-3,6-4 after which he beat

Murray 6-1 7-6, the final match of the day was Novak taking on Guillermo Canas. He was ranked 53 on the planet, Canas went down to Novak 6-1, 6-2, 6-1, and for the victory, Djokovic collected over half one million dollars.

Then, in late April Novak won a tournament for the second time during his World Tour event in Estoril, Portugal. Djokovic had been in great performance as his French Open approaching, but during the following two tournaments Spain's Nadal along with Carlos Moya defeated him in the quarterfinals. For the French Open, Djokovic played exceptionally excellently. At 6th place worldwide and he was among the top four players at the competition. Nikolay Davydenko and Federer were in one part of the draw, and Nole as well as Nadal on the other side. Rafa played on clay back at the time He beat Djokovic in three sets, and then taking on Federer to win the championship by four sets. Novak was hoping that when tennis turned to grass later it would give him an advantage hand.At Wimbledon in 2007, Djokovic was a tough opponent however he was able to win numerous games to make it to the semi-finals. The game was tied with just one set, which was Nadal winning the third set. injuries ended the match prematurely for Novak. "I was not sleeping through the night as I was suffering from lots of blood and other things, so I barely walked in the morning. I tried my best to make it onto the court since I was wondering whether I should go out and take part in a game? The situation was so serious." A injury to his foot that led to an aching back caused Novak to pull out. Finals went down to five sets. Federer won against Nadal.

Umag, Croatia, was an easy destination for Novak However, the outcome wasn't his best. Novak was beaten with Viktor Troicki in the second round. Viktor was ranked the 176th position; Novak was the world third-ranked player. The loss was shocking however, the tennis season was set to begin in North America, and there were plenty of opportunities for Djokovic.

In August, Montreal, Novak announced he was a top player by defeating all three of the players who were ranked ahead of Novak. Novak dropped to no. 4 on the planet. In Montreal Novak defeated all players with a ranking of 3-1. Novak was able to advance through the tournament and, to take the crown He defeated Andy Roddick, followed by Nadal and Federer during the final. Novak was disappointed in the next tournament, which was which was held in Cincinnati by Moya and then he travelled for his next event, the US Open with a lot of optimism. He faced Moya once more in the quarterfinals and defeated her in three sets. The next opponent was a Spaniard But this time it wasn't Nadal. Novak defeated David Ferrer in three sets. Djokovic was making his debut Grand Slam final. Federer beat the match in straight sets, however, it was a close match to the point that two ended in tiebreaks. Federer won 7-6, 7-6, 6-4.

Through this period of Novak's life, the public began to notice an increase in his "Djoker" persona. The character became popular due to the impersonations of tennis players. He was not only a student of the game with great attention to figure out strategies to beat his opponents However, he also analyzed numerous players in such a way that he was able to imitate every aspects of their sport. He had their walking and manners, as well as racquet swings perfect. However, it wasn't only Nadal or Federer He also mimicked Maria Sharapova and many other players both active and retired. He also altered his attire by pulling them up on his sleeves or shorts in order to appear like other players. He also utilized towels to alter the shape of his body in imitation of Serena Williams.

Novak was able to finish his year winning big which included a win in a tournament in Vienna as well as two games during Davis Cup play. However, what was not known back then was that he, along with others were requested to forfeit matches for the basis of. Later, Novak would explain what was going on: "I was not approached directly. I was contacted via people from my team. We discarded it out immediately. A person tried to contact me, didn't contact me directly. Nothing came of the conversation." It included a promise to pay $200,000 to forfeit a match in Russia however Novak did not play in that tournament. The money was not needed and he earned close to four million dollars just from the prize money in the year. In addition, he claimed that participating in this is "crime in sport."

Chapter 16: Winning the 2008 Australian Open

Since he was already in the Grand Slam final, there only one move to Novak to complete in order to be able to reach an Grand Slam final. It wasn't long before Novak to accomplish that goal; the following Grand Slam after the US Open was the 2008 Australian Open, and Djokovic seemed to be in good performance. He dominated his opponents with ease round-after-round. Hewitt as well as Ferrer were two of players that he eliminated. It was Novak playing in the semis the match in which Roger Federer was his opponent.

It was an entirely different Novak that those who played Federer earlier in his career. Novak was broken only twice during the game; Novak scored 78% of the points during his initial serve as well as he was more successful than Roger. First set was won by Novak with a score of 7-5. Novak did not give up in the second and took the set 3-1. The match was not as close in the third set however, Novak was victorious in the tiebreak. The result was an enormous Grand Slam chance for Djokovic in the same way that earlier Nadal was eliminated in the semifinal against the unseeded Frenchman Jo-Wilfried tsonga. To Serbian supporters this was significant due to another reason: his close friend Ana Ivanovic was in the finals of the women's tournament.

Ana revealed the length of time they'd been friends for: "We met each other in the year 2004, when we were just four years old. It was not even tennis back then. My dad and his uncle had a connection from the time of school, and so we played on the beach, and it's really very funny to watch him perform so well today. We also played a few tournaments including under-10s and under-12s when we were in Serbia. We then traveled in the same direction, so it's good to reconnect with each other, as well as having several real-life moments."

Maria Sharapova won the women's final the following year in Melbourne. Ivanovic was the winner of in the 2009 French Open. However, there was an excuse to feel happy during Melbourne: Djoko won. It didn't go according exactly as planned, since his opponent took the first set. With a ranking of 38, Tsonga surprised everyone by taking the opening set, at 6-4. Novak was victorious in the following two sets, winning 6-4 and 7-3. Novak was a dominant player. Frenchman had a big serve in the game; Novak had 15 aces to Novak's 11, while Djokovic played the best return game, and was extremely dominant in returning the second serve of his opponent. The fourth set was extremely competitive, however Novak was able to win 7-6 with his debut Grand Slam trophy. Novak also got a stuffed animal toy, as well as a cheque of $1,370,000.

After his biggest win in a tournament of his career Novak was a bit disappointed during the subsequent matches. He was eliminated from an Davis Cup match against Russia before he took his retirement. In the ATP tournament at Marseille He lost in the second round to Gilles Simon in the second round. Next was Dubai. He struggled in Dubai due to the scorching heat and time of when that the tournaments were played however, he managed to score three wins, before losing against Andy Roddick. Nole took the title in his first tournament at the Indian Wells event, defeating Nadal in the semifinals, and Mardy Fish at the end of the tournament. However, he later lost to Andy Roddick at the final in Miami after Kevin Anderson beat him 7-6 3-4, 7-6, 3-6, 6-4.

The ATP Masters Series returned to Europe this year, and it was Novak against the top two tennis players over three matches. Federer won against Nole at Monte Carlo when Djokovic retired in the second game. Novak took the title in the Rome competition, but was defeated by Nadal during the finals in Hamburg. Novak was not waiting too long to have another chance against Nadal however, it was through the clay courts playing surface at Roland Garros. Novak needed to put in a lot of effort during the opening round. Novak lost his first set against Denis

Gremelmayr before winning in four sets. Then, he defeated all of his rivals in straight sets, advancing to the semis. Nadal, who is the master of clay was waiting for Novak, however, and Novak fell 6-4, 6-1 7-6. The clay wasn't the only thing Nadal was a master at, however. Just a few days later, on Queen's, Nadal again defeated Djokovic with Straight sets at the end of the match.

When she played Wimbledon at the 2008 Wimbledon, Nole suffered a shocking loss. Just a few years prior, Marat Safin was too tall and experienced as Novak was just beginning his tennis career. In this case, it was Safin with a ranking of 75, but was defeated by Djokovic during the 2nd round of the known Grand Slam in history. Djokovic later lost to Great Britain, and in the next two Masters Series events, he fell to British's Andy Murray. The next time he competed, Novak would be playing for his home country.

Most tennis tournaments state that it's impossible to win a tournament even if you lose. In August of 2008, Novak was able to do just this. This was during an event called the Olympic Games in Beijing, China And while Novak did fall short in a game at the end of the competition however, he still managed to participate in another game for an Olympic medal. As a player for Serbia at the time, he began his tournament with victories over one American and an American, a German as well as the Russian as well as an Frenchman. If he was to have a shot to win the gold medal the Serbian had to defeat the best tennis player in Spain, Rafael Nadal. It was actually the competition for this prize, since the opposite side of the draw was pretty much and open. Federer had a rough time with James Blake in the quarters but then Blake fell to Fernando Gonzalez of Chile. Nadal beat Novak the next day, and he won 6-1, 6-4. Novak was able to win the prize, but he then was able to beat Blake for bronze. Nadal took the title in the final, as expected. Federer took home the gold medal in doubles.

The US Open was something that caused Novak noticeably spotted, as well as the crowd cheered. It started off very well for Novak who easily defeated Arnaud Clement as well as Robert Kendrick. Then he was pushed to the limit to the limit by Marin Cilic and Tommy Robredo. The result was an opponent in the quarterfinals, Roddick who fans backed and was mentioned prior to the game that Djokovic could have faked injury sometimes. Novak was victorious in the first two sets, however Roddick won the third. In the fourth, Roddick tried to take into a decisive set, but he lost his momentum due to two double errors as well as Novak was victorious by winning a tiebreak in the 4th set. Afterward, Djokovic celebrated and said certain things that the crowd did not like. The crowd booed him.

Roddick discussed his experience after their game: "I was talking trash then he walked out to beat my pants off of me in the contest] just like he did, and afterwards, he kind of chirped. Then he walks straight into the locker roomto the locker room]. I went straight toward him, and set him against his locker. However, I noticed the trainer of his was just a smaller that Donovan and I thought about it." Federer beat Djokovic in the semi-finals. Nadal in that moment was the world's number. 1. He lost to Murray in the semi-final after which Federer took the title in the title in the final.

For some fans of tennis, Novak was seen as a antagonist. They could come up with a multitude of explanations as to why they felt that manner. There was a belief that he called trainers too often as well as that the tactic was employed to disrupt his opposition. There was also a claim that he was a loser in matches due to having to retire on numerous occasions. The fans were accustomed to playing the Nadal and Federer performance, and they were not happy by the fact that Novak was there and beat either of them or both in the course of a tournament. The Novak family was not a fan of Federer at the time, and in those days, Roger wasn't impressed with Novak and the way he chose to quit playing: "I think he's a joke, you know, when it comes down to his injuries."

Following a couple of more tournaments, Novak went to China to compete in the Tennis Masters Cup. Novak made it through the round-robin stages by winning two times and suffering losing to make the finals. He received the prize cash prize of $1,240,000 for beating Gilles Simon and then Nikolay Davydenko in the final.

Chapter 17: Chasing Feeder

The year 2009 wasn't a good year for Novak and it could have been the same for many tennis players. However, Djokovic was not able to achieve what was his goal. His opening match of 2009 ended in an unanticipated loss against Latvia's Ernests Gulbis in straight sets in Brisbane. As he moved south towards Sydney He lost his final against the Finnish Jarkko Nieminen. The next stop was Melbourne Novak, who Novak had the unique situation at that time. He was in the circumstance of being a defending champion at the Grand Slam.

The Australian Open was not an enjoyable moment for Novak during the Australian Open. It was hot and hard in the heat, and for him to make it to the quarterfinals he needed be playing to 2:26 early at dawn to beat Marcos Baghdatis. It was then a scorching tennis match with a player that he doesn't particularly enjoy playing, Andy

Roddick. Roddick was victorious in the 4th set after Novak was forced to retire due to hot temperatures. "I've been through a few retirements, but always on the basis of a reason or since I believed I couldn't continue. Today, I tried my best. But it's not always easy to fight the inside of your body."

Many statistics were prepared when it came to discussing Novak. He played in 17 Grand Slams and quit four times. The time was when no one Federer, Nadal nor Murray were ever retiring during in a Grand Slam match. That was an issue Novak was required to tackle in order to become the top player of all time and it would not happen in a short time.

It was not a big issue the next month; Novak won the Dubai tournament. Novak was able to win a lot of tennis matches, but had no tournaments in some time. The next tournament he won was one that stood out to his name, Serbia Open in 2009. Serbia Open. Novak has transferred his participation in the Dutch Open to Belgrade, as did his uncle Goran Djokovic was the tournament's director. Novak was given a break in the opening round and following that lost to Serbians Janko Tipsarevic, and Viktor Troicki. After he beat Italian Andreas Seppi, he made it to the final. World No. 3 Novak against world No. 179 Lukasz Kubot of Poland. The result was expected as the Serbian crowd booed at the time Novak took his Serbia Open final 6-3, 7-6.

It was the French Open was a disappointment and he was eliminated to Philipp Kohlschreiber in round three. against Philipp Kohlschreiber. Wimbledon was not much better, because Novak fell to Tommy Haas in the quarterfinals. In the end, Federer beat Djokovic during the US Open semifinals. Five titles, and over five million dollars wasn't bad year for Novak however, he was looking for much more. Novak wouldn't be able to get it in 2010 either.

He returned to Australia in the beginning of 2010 although he did not quit, he didn't enjoy himself, perhaps he would have been able to retire in an event. In the quarterfinals the match ended in defeat to Tsonga 7-6, 6-7 6-1, 1-6, 6-3 and became very sick. "After two sets (of four sets) I needed to use the bathroom. I was unable to hold it. It was impossible to hold on. In other words, if I did not do it, I'd vomit on the court. It was this horrible sensation. In the event that you've lost a significant amount of fluids and the engine fails it's what I felt. I was very slow using my legs during the fourth and during the 5th set. I couldn't get his feet down to the baseline. This was my biggest issue."

The Dr. Igor Cetojevic was one of the many Serbs looking at Djokovic on TV in Europe after he was eliminated from the match in the Australian Open. Contrary to the majority of viewers, he believed that he had the ability to help Novak. He believed Novak was suffering from a problem in his digestion. They were to meet during July, and Djokovic changed his eating habits. He would consume fewer meals, and eliminate dairy products and gluten in his diet. And although Djokovic was lighter in weight, the player would be still strong and impressive with his tennis racquet.

The doctor joined Novak's Team which was the name Novak used to describe his team of family and friends who helped him. They would go on a journey around the globe over the course of a year or two. Since this time, the doctor has revealed his findings and treatment strategies: "I found that he was extremely allergic to gluten, a gluten-based protein found in wheat, one of the main food items in the diet of Novak's. He was a child, as the majority of young people regularly eating wheat-based food items like pizza, bread as well as pasta and pancakes. He was an excellent student who followed my suggestions and getting excellent grades."

Great results were expected for Novak during 2011, however Novak still managed to achieve some results during 2010. Even though there were no Grand Slam wins, he was able to win victories at Dubai as well as Beijing. In the semis of Wimbledon, Novak achieved a World ranking of 2. The biggest achievement this year did not involve cost or of any nature; it was a matter of nationalism.

Djokovic won the Davis Cup for Serbia. The Serbian was joined by Viktor Troicki, Janko Tipsarevic and Nenad Zimonjic. However, when you consider Novak taking every singles game that he took part in, he certainly get the credit. In the first Davis Cup event was Serbia in the match against USA in which Novak won two matches easily. After Wimbledon, Novak won two games against Croatian players, both of whom were placed in the top 20. Following Djokovic defeated Tomas Berdych and the Czech Republic in the semi-finals, the final was between Serbia and France winning the title. The site was Belgrade and that was a major advantage to Serbia. Djokovic returned to be the third-ranked player worldwide in his first match, when he beat Gilles Simon. Serbia was beaten in a singles and doubles tournament the match was the responsibility of Novak to ensure they were in the game. He succeeded by beating Gael Monfils, 6-2, 6-2 or 7-5. Viktor Troicki beat Michael Llodra in the final match and Serbia was the winner of it the Davis Cup.

As with many tennis players, Novak chose to live in Monaco. Novak quit Serbia because of a number of reasons however, while the main attraction is the fact that there's no tax on income in Monaco but there were additional reasons that were mentioned. Novak could list a few reasons for them "[Privacy is] among reasons that I'm staying away from my home with my family in Serbia as I do not want to be a burden on my family. This is what I was looking for and was able to find that in Monaco. I feel so happy having spent time in Monaco." It was some things that he didn't miss from his country of birth in his own words, "I miss a lot of things in SerbiaI miss a lot about Serbia. I'm craving my food, my family members in general, as well as my friends from there who I do not get to meet frequently, however currently I'd rather be somewhere and not there."

Chapter 18: Ranked number 1. In 2011's Grand Slams, since Novak took the title at the Australian Open in 2008, the Australian Open, and up until the close of 2010 the majority of them were held either Federer and Nadal. Juan Martin del Potro had won the title of surprise at this year's US Open. If Djokovic would like to take down these two legendary players He would need raise his game even greater level than the one he'd been playing at and this is precisely the way he went about it.

The year 2009 could have been Federer's Year, as he took home two Grand Slams, and was at the semi-finals of two others. The year 2010 may be referred to as the Year of Nadal as he also was the winner of 3 Grand Slams. However, 2011 was the year of Djokovic. The Serbian tennis player started the year, just as every tennis player does each year in Australia.

Novak was able to overcome any obstacles in advancing to the opening round in the 2010 Australian Open. In the quarterfinals he beat Berdych 6-1 7-6 6-1. In the semis the Serbian defeated Federer 7-6 7-5 and 6-4. In the final, against Andy Murray, it was Djokovic who had the edge in the match, and Murray did not seem to be prepared for his big win. Novak almost broke his first serve, as well as with Murray inability to win many first serves on the court which meant Novak was able to slash his second serve with devastating return. This resulted in a Novak win, 6-4 6-1 and 7-3.

The results of all matches in the early months of 2011 had Novak winning. Following Australia Novak was victorious at Dubai against Federer, Indian Wells over Nadal, Miami over Nadal, Belgrade over Feliciano Lopez Then Madrid and Rome in which, each time, Nadal couldn't stop him during the final. The court was also a winner both on clay and hardcourts.

The streak came to its end with French clay. Novak did manage to win five games but lost in the French Open semifinal against Federer with four sets. As he entered Wimbledon, Novak was confident that he would be able to keep his streak to continue. In the final, he was forced to compete to earn the place and played three games which went to four sets which included a difficult semifinal match against Tsonga. The final match was Nole against Rafa. Five games in front to 4 in the initial match, Novak broke Nadal's serve through great forehands, and an impressive backhand. In the second, Novak took a swell of skill and confidence and dominated the match 6-1. In the third, the match was dominated by Nadal. Since Nadal the Spaniard took the final game of the set, without Novak scoring a point there was speculation that Djokovic may not be successful. It didn't happen. Novak took the set in the fourth by 6-3. This was the first time he won a Wimbledon victory.

Djokovic ate grass on Centre Court to celebrate. He was extremely happy about the outcome: "This is my favorite tournament. It was the one that I've always dreamed of winning and the very first one I've ever seen throughout my entire life. I'm sure I'm not in bed, and I'm having the dream of my life. If you're playing the top tennis player on earth, Rafael Nadal, who has taken home two of the past three Wimbledons and who has always won the major match against me during these Grand Slams you have to perform at the highest level of my level. I needed to be at my very best."

The next stop came North America, and he came to the planet as was not yet. 1. He took the title the event in Montreal He fell to Murray in the finals of the Cincinnati competition. The Flushing Meadows crowd would be his next challenge. He had already won two Grand Slams. And in order to get to win a third, he'd have to beat all the players they adored. He took five sets, however he defeated Federer in the semi-final match. In the final match, he was up against Nadal. Novak is still playing in his prime and lost only one set. But the tiebreak was lost. Nole won the match Nole beating 6-4, 6-2 7-6, 6-1.

When Novak's successes kept piling in the series, the focused on him and journalists and even fans frequently spoke about the fact that the ball bounced often before serving. Up to fifteen or even twenty times, the amount the times that Novak bounced his ball prior to serving was a source of irritation for certain players and even fans. Mind games are an integral element of the game and, If Novak used it in order to gain an advantage, he probably did it several times. The bounces were counted by the players as well, and Novak probably did as well: "My record was in 2007 in the Davis Cup against Australia. I had the ball bounce 308 or three instances (before playing)."

This was an excellent year for Novak. He won $12,595,903. He was the winner of the majority of his games. He added 10 more title to the trophy collection. Novak has a record-breaking streak of wins with 31 wins over consecutive Masters matches. He also had an unbroken streak of 43 tennis match victories. Novak won the title in three Grand Slams before progressing into the semifinals of one. He was awarded the number. one ranking in the world. Novak did it all.

The health aspect was one that Novak could count on. Even though he experienced two retirements throughout the course of the season, he saw seven competitors retire, and hand the win. A new way of eating resulted in the energy he had never experienced prior to. Breakfast was about energy "Your body requires sugar. Particularly, it requires fructose which is the sugar you find in a variety of fruits and vegetables as well as honey." The man would finish his each day with a new need: "At night, I have no to be energized. At dinner I'll say to my body that I need you to get rid of the mess that I created. You must eat this protein and take care of what needs to be completed.'" Novak was willing to experiment with new techniques to maintain his fitness which included his controversial CVAC pod, which appeared like an egg-like structure that was inside while he was able to simulate high-altitude conditions as well as various other activities that can help build an individual's body.

Chuck Norris, Jean-Claude Van Damme, Arnold Schwarzenegger, Sylvester Stallone and Novak Djokovic filmed a movie in the year 2011, and it was scheduled to be released in August 2012. Unfortunately for Novak the film, his performance was cut off from the editing room floor. If a different and longer edition of The Expendables 2 is released and Djokovic's fans are interested in combating bad guys using his tennis racquet need to look on the Internet for a short video. Novak was in Bulgaria for the shoot in the final scene of the movie, featuring a massive fight in an airport terminal. Being the only actor not acknowledged in an Chuck Norris movie could mean Novak is a possibility for the big screen as one of the first times Liam Neeson appeared in major films was as an uncredited character in The Delta Force, a Chuck Norris movie The Delta Force.

Chapter 19: Battling Feeder, Murray and Nodal

It was becoming an ongoing trend for Djokovic and he began the season with a huge win. He dropped less than 10 games in total to make it through the initial three rounds at the 2012 Australian Open. Novak was then able to beat the local favorite Hewitt after which he defeated Ferrer with straight sets. There were only two games remaining in the tournament which resulted in 10 sets for Novak. The semi-final lasted nearly five hours. Novak beat Murray 6-1, 3-6 7-5, 6-7, 6-1. It was actually a shorter tennis match, and the final went on more than six hours. Nadal had a desire for the title, as was Novak was aiming for the world no. one ranking was a bit off, but did not make it the cut. The final result of the epic, record-breaking match was Djokovic beating 6-4, 5-7 7-5, 6-2 7-5. With five hours and 53 minutes, it was the longest final game in every Grand Slam. Serbian basketball legend Vlade Divac was in attendance in support of Djokovic.

The semifinals were lost against Murray in Dubai as well as to John Isner in Indian Wells, but another victory was claimed by Novak after he once again took over the court in Miami. Novak defeated Murray in the court's hardcourt and then lost to Nadal in the clay courts of Monte Carlo. The moment when the French Open came around, Novak could have the opportunity to be an official Grand Slam champion of all four events at one however everyone was aware that Nadal was determined to thwart this. In the beginning it appeared that Novak would not make it to the finals during the finals of 2012 French Open; he was forced to play five sets against Seppi as well as Tsonga. In the semifinals, his opponent was Federer however, Novak beat Federer in three sets. Nadal did not disappoint to win, just like everyone else, for the final. Nadal won with four sets.

England was always the centre of tennis in the globe, but in 2012 the importance of this sport was increased. It was not just that England be hosting Wimbledon like every year however, the London Olympics were also scheduled to follow the event. Novak wanted to experience victory, and grass once more, on the most prestigious tennis court. Djokovic was thought to be among one of the top players in the world. But, even though Roger Federer was getting older He was still capable of beating any player. He was the most dominant of Novak during the Wimbledon semi-final. After that, it was on to the Summer Olympics. Novak was the one to carry the flag of Serbia as well as their hopes for winning a tennis gold. He faced an old rival in the second round Andy Roddick, and won 6-1, 6-2. In the final match, Novak was up against Andy Murray, and Murray took 7-5, 7-5. Novak could still have a shot of winning a medal but Novak would place fourth in the competition having lost the final to Juan Martin del Potro in the bronze medal match. In the past Novak had, however, Novak had received a award for his effort which was it was the Karadjordjeva Star Medal, which was awarded to Novak by Serbia to commemorate all that he has accomplished for Serbia.

After Wimbledon as well as the Olympics There were many occasions that Novak to take part in during 2012. He won another four of them. For instance, the US Open was not one of them. Andy Murray got the win by five sets during the final, beating Novak. Djokovic won events that took place in Toronto, Beijing and Shanghai and also winning the ATP World Tour Finals in London. In the end, he was World No. 1.

The 2013 season didn't start as the same as last year's; it was actually a repeated. The player went to Australia and clinched yet another Grand Slam. Then he took home Dubai yet again. He was also a winner in a couple of Davis Cup matches, as well. Then, he made a statement with his performance. Nadal has won 8 consecutive Monte Carlo Opens however he wasn't able to make it nine. Nadal made it to the finals, however Djokovic beat him 6-2 and 7-6. The result provided Novak confidence that he had the chance to be victorious in the French final, however that did not happen, since Nadal took revenge in the semifinals and won. At one point crucial to the match Novak was pushed into the net and, as the net was touched and smashed it, he was automatically disqualified from the point. Djokovic was not happy, even though it's written in the rulebook.

Wimbledon followed, and Novak did not lose a single set during his run to the semi-finals. Then, he lost two sets against del Potro before advancing to the final. It was a historic result and not exactly as Novak was hoping for: Andy Murray won 6-4 7-5 6-1, 7-5, 6-4. In the US Open was also a disappointing one for Novak and he made it into the final however, Rafael Nadal defeated his opponent and swept the tournament 6-2 6-1, 3-6, 6-4.

This final in New York City would be the only defeat Djokovic suffered in 2013. Novak was victorious in the tournaments of Beijing, Shanghai and Paris and also his first ever ATP World Tour Finals when Novak defeated world No. 1 Rafa Nadal. In addition to Novak winning matches in tennis and getting engaged, but he was also engaged.

Few tennis players are with no rituals and things to complete in their lives, which for

Novak the most important thing is to drink water. Even though Novak plays in the summer months however, he isn't drinking what is expected. "Water is essential to the success in the body's process for healing. However, I do not drink the consumption of ice water. If you consume ice water, your body requires to supply additional blood to the digestive system to warm the water up to 98.6 degrees. This takes blood away from the place I need it to be, which is inside my muscle." The man is one who consumes lots of fruits, particularly bananas.

There was a change in the beginning of 2014 The reason was that not only did he have an absence of Australian Open tournament win, and he was not even in the semis. Wawrinka beat Novak in the quarterfinals however, it took five sets, and the match in the final was 9-7. Following that, Federer beat Djokovic in

Dubai however Novak beat Roger during the final match of Indian Wells, and soon following, there was another victory at the Miami tournament, but this time over Nadal during the championship. There was a minor dispute prior to this match at Miami during a game against Murray. Novak was able to reach over the net but wasn't allowed to strike the ball, and get the point. Murray was unhappy. In Monte Carlo, Federer eliminated Novak however, Nole won against Nadal during the semi-final of Rome.

The following two tournaments included Grand Slams. Novak will play Rafa as well as Roger during the final match. In France playing in clay, Nadal defeated Djokovic 3-6 7-5 6-2 7-5, 6-4. Then, at Wimbledon, Federer gave it all he had, but Novak's time came as well as a change in the guard in tennis. Djokovic took the title in five sets and scored a score of 6-7, 4-4, 7-6 7, 6-4. Novak was also the world's number. 1.

The day of his wedding in 2014 might have been more significant for Novak than his previous victories on the tennis courts. "Seeing her for the first time in her wedding dress, smiling and walking towards me, she looked like an angel," Novak told his wife Jelena Ristic. The wedding took place at Sveti Stefan resort in Montenegro. Sveti Stefan Resort located in Montenegro were attended by Boris Becker, Janko Tipsarevic, Marian Vajda, Viktor Troicki as well as other relatives and close friends.

www.ingramcontent.com/pod-product-compliance
Lightning Source LLC
Chambersburg PA
CBHW070734020526
44118CB00035B/1343